THE MARK
OF THE BEAST

THE MARK OF THE BEAST
WHAT IS MANKIND?

BILLY WILSON

iUniverse®

THE MARK OF THE BEAST
WHAT IS MANKIND?

iUniverse books may be ordered through booksellers or by contacting:

iUniverse
1663 Liberty Drive
Bloomington, IN 47403
www.iuniverse.com
1-800-Authors (1-800-288-4677)

ISBN: 978-1-5320-3902-7 (sc)
ISBN: 978-1-5320-3901-0 (e)

Library of Congress Control Number: 2018900065

Print information available on the last page.

iUniverse rev. date: 01/09/2018

FOREWORD

I am trying hard to wake a few of us up. I have spent what little savings I had in the past five years getting these books printed and published. I would recommend to anybody that is raising children or planning to live a few more years to read some in these books. "Killing Self" ---- "What is God's word?" "Revealing a Righteous God" ---- "Mystery Babylon" ---- "The Mark Of the Beast" vs "The Spiritual Language of God"

Jesus was slain to become worthy to take the book from God on the throne and break the seals thereof to redeem the creation and the intents from the father. He did not receive all power and authority from God until he gave his body back for a sacrifice worthy to receive the creation and men as the son of God who became born of women and flesh, died and gave his blood and body back for the price of mankind out of every kindred and tongue and people and nation. And has made us unto our God kings and priest, and we shall reign on the earth.

Many angels cheered as a lamb stood as it had been slain, with seven horns, seven eyes, which are the seven Spirits of God sent forth into all the earth, poured out the prayers of the saints. Every creature in heaven, on the earth, under the earth, such as are in the sea, and all that are in them. Heard I saying, blessing, and honor, and power be unto him that sitteth upon the throne and unto the lamb forever and ever.

#ONE

In the book of revelations that Jesus gave to John while on the thirteen-square mile rock the Bible calls the Isle of Patmos. John was told to write it down, he did.

John saw an Angel flying in the midst, of heaven, having the everlasting Gospel to preach unto them that dwell on the earth, every nation, and kindred, tongue and people. That included every man on the earth.

The "Mark of the Beast" is first mentioned in the thirteenth chapter of the book of Revelations, one of the books John wrote, the last book in the Bible. The Mark of the Beast is identified as a mark in the forehead or in one's hands, the name of the beast, the number of his name. It is the number of a man, 6-6-6, God says man power without God is a beast. God's number is seven. The beast will never make that number.

We are told to be able to establish every word with at least two or three witnesses from the Word of God, before it can be repeated as a gospel word, as to the way it is used. This would make it a Spiritual Language Word as the Bible is written in. This being soundly and thoroughly practiced, would eliminate every denomination but one on the earth. It would be the established Word of God, by the Word of God. Same as the Bible.

Man is an amazingly complicated piece of machinery created and operated by the Spirit of God, and given the power to reproduce himself and a free will. From the beginning man has sought to take total control of himself and everything around him in every way. He has made much progress in these last few years, but will not be able to attain complete control until he can overpower God. He will never do that. Lucifer tried that once.

Man's age started out being like a thousand years old in the beginning of man on this earth. After about three cuts, God cut man's time to live on this earth down to seventy years old in King David's time, around three to four thousand years ago. With all of man's success and accomplishments added together man has not added one year to his average length of life since it was shortened down for mankind in David's time, though he thinks he has. Man can figure his average age in years around today, but he cannot read and believe the Bible. When it is right ever time.

God has named and describe the total beginning and end to all mankind, and most of everything in between. Man was built and blessed with a great desire and ambition to take control of everything on the earth. God has given him a free will and in charge of all things, if he does not cross someone else's same freedom as he has, and will acknowledge God as the head. This was one of God's common-sense laws as well as an order.

Man turned out with such a provocative greedy nature, God was forced to intervein. He has no intention of saving mankind in the shape man has gotten himself into. Man is destined to annihilate himself, by the desire for himself to sit in God's seat. God's intention is to save only a few out of all mankind to be with him forever, those who have overcome their provocative nature, called carnal, anything apart from the Spirit of God.

If you are not happy here with God being the head, do not expect him to take you to be with him forever. I do not believe that to be a bullish attitude considering how plain an explanation he has given to us. And what he has plainly spoken and offered to prepare for mankind that can love righteousness. If a man will not love and receive righteousness in his short tenner here, he will be destroyed in hell. Might remember that the next time you start complaining and griping to God, and accusing him.

It is the same Spirit in us now as it will be that will be operating in us throughout eternity. If we will align it with the Spirit of God, or else it will align with the Antichrist. If we cannot acknowledge God's Spirit as the head here, how will we love it on the other side? It is a righteous Spirit, God will tolerate nothing else to be with him. One third of the spirits that God created in heaven, rebelled and left God, we have that for an example. If we accept their spirit here they will be the ones we will spend eternity with. For sure they will all be burned up at the end.

I can assure you if spirits are torturing you here, they are not the spirits that God's Spirit has sent to us. Even though it is a practice of mankind to blame God with everything that is unpleasant to his own carnal nature which is aligned with the one-third that Michael kicked out of heaven and you are believing and catering to them. They do not love anything that is righteous, and cannot tell the truth. God's Word tells us of a better Spirit, we must believe and accept him to see it. Carnality cannot see a spirit, we must believe the Spirit of God. God says every Word of his is Truth, but man's word is a lie unless it aligns with what God says, then it is God's Word. The only Spirit of God we can have, is now in his Spiritual Language he gave to the world.

We are each given a spirit of our own and are told to train it up in the fear and admonition of the Lord and let the Spirit of God lead us, it will never lead us against the Word of God which is the King James Authorized Translation of the Bible. Jesus, gave it to England, around sixteen-hundred AD, said it was him in Word form. He does not want a word changed or nothing taken out of a word in it. If it has, then it is not God's Word, or God's Spiritual Language. I intend to write more on this subject in this book.

It is the only thing on earth that is going into heaven unchanged when Christ comes back for his. It is already Spiritual, just the Language of Words that can be found in the King James Translation of the Bible, they are Jesus Christ. One can ride them through the complete change, all the way over but he must be born again into the Spirit of God to understand that Language. The carnal cannot have that and will stay in the carnal world. And will ever be locked out from the presents of the Father.

I write a lot about being led by the Spirit, it is what the Bible is about. God demands it, without any doubt it calls for us to come to know something about the Spirit of God. Without it, we are referred to by our creator as being dumb, blind, dead, lost, and without hope, and many other things, like having been turned over to our lust after carnal things. His Spirit cannot be obtained without some studying, believing, and receiving. We cannot be saved without it. I have done much of all of them, and would like to share some of it with you.

The best I can figure out, the spirit is the same thing in our bodies as the brain and nervous system, making up our minds. Together, they operate and control our entire body, giving us complete responsibility for our decisions and actions if we have a sound Godly mind. *Sound* implies, not having any holes and hollow spots in it and having a firm foundation under it, like two good feet and strong legs and can stand against opposition, with a sound voice.

I have been hearing, from reliable sources, that our scientists have about gotten a mechanical system ready to start installing it into all human beings. They say it can outperform all the things that a normal human can do. Think, plan, see-ahead, and make choses and decisions with its own will. The Bible tells us about the same thing. If you don't believe that, then tell me who the people are that are running to the mountains, praying for the rocks and mountains to fall on them and hide them from the face of *"The one that is sitting on the throne,"* told about there in Revelations, chapter nine. When Jesus is pouring out God's wrath upon the earth trying to get, what is left of mankind, to repent and receive the Spirit of God.

It is certainly not God's Spirit-filled people. But death will flee from them for a five-month period. Jesus is pleading with them, with his wrath of torcher, to repent. Even though it will mean death to the carnal man created body that has received the Mark of a Man, when they do. Jesus will be set-up in Jerusalem with his saints and the Jews ruling the earth with an iron hand. It is not any different from the agreement we've had with God all along.

The carnal flesh has always been required to die-out for God to accept anyone into his Spirit. This "Mark of the Beast" is a covenant to accept the Mark of a man permanently, and death to withdraw from it. Spiritually speaking, if the flesh would die out now, we could go on living in it but the Spirit of God is to have complete control. The Mark of the Beast is a contract, marked into the flesh and mind, once you receive it you cannot take it out and live. The flesh has agreed to not do that; then it must physically die to receive the Spirit of God.

My Bible speaks of such a creature, calls it the "Mark of the Beast." I am getting a book published now written on this subject, calling it revealing the "Mark of the Beast" by tittle. Don't expect me to explain how it works but I can say a few words on how the body works and these scientists will have to build a computer to control a man's thinking, or his mind, to accomplish this project. Our thinking, controls our spirit and our body. Our mind controls our thinking. It is hard to tell what someone without a sound mind, is thinking, he is unstable for sure.

The spirit is the life of anything that has life in it. When the spirit has left something, it is dead, dead. These scientists know, to put life into anything, they must come up with a spirit, so they have been working twenty-four-seven to come up with a computer that will replace a spirit. Since they cannot create a spirit in anything, they will use one's spirit and one's mind to control the computer while it is controlling the mind. Called the "Mark of the Beast" (Man without God is a beast) I can see no better way to explain it. It is kind of like a dog chasing its tail, around and around, think they can have it winning? They think so.

God says this will, in a short time, put an end to all normal flesh. Scientist are saying the same thing. God will not accept any such people that has accepted a man-made and controlled spirit, made and controlled by man's hands and the spirit of Lucifer. Man must deny this spirit, and accept the Spirit of God. If one accepts this "Mark of the Beast" it will be accepting the death penalty for our bodies. God teaches this.

If one lives down to the time, of the rule of the *Antichrist*, he gives one the choice to take the mark or he will take one's head. One might as well give him their head, in the end it will be the same thing either way. The majority, of people today have been taught they do not need the Spirit of God, or the Language of the Spirit. Kind of pitiful any way one can describe it, if they do not receive the Spirit of God they have no real life in them, just an image of the real thing. The image will be controlled by the mark once it has taken it.

This is the same deal from the beginning. When Adam and Eve disobeyed God, they died, God has tried to find a way to reconcile man back to him ever since. The ones he wants. Man is looking for a way to bar Christ (Which is God) out of any control of his body. This *mark* will be it, but a fatal move for the body of man.

The "Mark of the Beast" is introduced in the thirteenth chapter of Revelations. It, and the next three chapters, will about cover the very end times up to the time of God's wrath. When the last seven-years-week, of the seventy-years of weeks told about in Daniel, is poured out on the earth. God will have turned back to the Jews with his saints, ruling from Jerusalem. Like he said he would do in Matthew twenty-four. It seems to me like the only way for anyone to receive the Spirit after one has taken this mark, is to give his body as a sacrifice for it.

I believe, from the writing, that the ones that has accepted Christ by this time, went with him back to the Jews. Like he told about in the twenty-forth chapter of the book of Matthew. The closest thing I can find in my Bible to what they call a rapture. They had accepted being a Jew when they accepted Christ. Seems very plain, that this consists of much more than the today's average Christians wants to accept or hear anything about. I am sure there is coming a time when one will not be hardly able to live on this earth without the presents of the people and the Spirit of Jesus Christ to protect one.

We do not see much deep studying of the Bible in the way God said to study it.

Did you ever wonder why Christ dwelt so much on his people to come together as one and get along and help each other? Because it is very necessary, I believe it is a must if we are going to make it. This has become much more important to God in these last days, and seems less important to man. Mostly because of man's so many inventions and fast and free living that man has chosen for himself and does not have time for God. Until he gets to thinking he has passed God up and God is just kind of getting in man's way.

God has said plainly, "Whosoever exalts himself, shall be abased." God teaches that very few will make it through these last days, and stay saved. I believe he teaches at the very end there will not be a one left alive and saved, except the ones that are with him and the Jews there at Jerusalem at a place called Armageddon. When God saves any Gentiles, after the mark, he will take them home at that time. The Antichrist world will make sure of that.

Christ is accepting the Jews for they have cried out for him to save them, and they have accepted him, while the gentiles have accepted the Antichrist and have killed the ones among them that will not. And have went after the Jews to kill them, Christ came back to save them, and will. The Mark of the Beast is the final last straw to living and controlling your own body.

Christ has said death is more blessed than the mark. Having Christ *now*, is better than either one. I was hoping and praying more earnest preachers would give the Mark of the Beast a more deeper study. As it is very possible that a few children born today may be living in the day of the Mark of the Beast. They sure can use some more in-depth information to help them to keep our country as free from it as possible. I believe Christ has said it is time we started preaching it, and from the Bible. Instead of so much preaching on how talented and comfortable man's inventions are than what God give to us.

Trump is a man sent from God to give this nation a chance to turn back to God. Trump cannot save us but he is there to give us a chance to turn back to Jesus while we still can, if we want to. I strongly believe that Trump is this country's last chance. Seems to me that the dumbest man on this earth should be able to see that, but God has said we are fools and blind, and we go on every day proving him right.

I started to write, I cannot understand that, but that would be wrong, I spent thirty some-odd years wrapped up in sin before I received Christ forty years ago and have not been sorry for one minute of it since. I not only gave up many things of the world, I gave up all the world and everything in it. I believe that was a good trade, for eternal life with God. And it's looking like, with my whole family, I am promised just that. He has saved my children and all my grandchildren from the world many times. It is looking favorable that they will all be saved when they leave this world.

This last seven years' week, will Lead up to the millennial reign, when Christ will set-up his kingdom there in Jerusalem for the millennial reign over the earth. Then the earth will have a perfect rule for a thousand years coming from Jesus Christ, with his martyrs and his saints ruling with him for one thousand years. (in this event, Jerusalem, Armageddon, the valley of Jehoshaphat, and a few other names, implies the same location.) The False Prophet and the Antichrist will have been thrown into hell and the Devil will be bound in chains of darkness in the pit with a thousand-year seal upon him. Christ did all that when he came back to save the Jews from Mystery Babylon there at Rome. That would cover some of the wars Jesus talked about. The fighting wars and killings.

The Devil will be released after the one thousand-year reign, to go over ever nation of the world to gather the ones that does not love righteousness, for the great battle of Armageddon, also called the day of the great battle of God Almighty.

To try to defeat Christ and his small camp of saints there in Jerusalem. Where Christ has been ruling with an iron hand. This appears to me to be maybe the first time Christ and Lucifer will meet face to face in an all-out battle. Lucifer will have a surprise coming, his ticket to hell for eternity.

They have had need of nothing but power and authority for and over themselves. They should know that has never worked. Christ took over to keep them from ending all flesh, to save the ones that loves righteousness. You can look over the world today and see how few that is going to be. They love self instead, and self is not righteous. Don't ever get to thinking that it is. Even when a computer brain can compute maybe a million times faster than a normal brain can, and more accurate. Part of the Markings of the Beast.

The time, of these events or, the length of their happenings, is not given plain in the scriptures. How long it will take Satan to go over the earth and raise, and I would suppose, gather and train, the largest army ever gathered on the earth, to meet around the valley of Jehoshaphat, I have no idea, but it will be a space and time to fulfil a lot of scripture that the Bible describes. Wars, killings, bloodshed like has never been seen before. I believe you can read about some of that in Joel. Maybe a little in about every book of the Bible.

The Devil will convince them that are left, they can defeat Jesus easily, with the largest army every gathered on the earth. Christ's little group probably don't even have a gun. Believe me, Christ has been rough on them in the world, trying to get them to repent. Then they will not need a gun, they will have Christ. It will be called the battle of Armageddon. Also called the day of the great battle of God almighty.

In this era of the Bible, many things we do not know of now, will have to be dealt with, like Robot human beings, and many other odd things, like making fire come down from heaven in sight of men. Sounds like the world's population will be built back up tremendously in the thousand-year millennial reign. Probably they will be given a chance to receive the Mark of the Beast or death in around this period. When Satan will be released for a period.

God will have judged the earth but will set up the white throne judgment to reward every person for their works, good or bad. Christ will throw Satan into the lake of fire where the False Prophet and the Antichrist already are, along with every soul that does not have its name written in the Lamb's Book of Life. The final separation. And will burn up the entire creation except the ones that are prepared to spend eternity with him. God has promised the Jews eternal reproduction. I don't know just how that will work out. But I believe every Gentile that plans to be in eternity with Christ better be prepared to completely be transformed over to being a Jew somewhere along the line.

This will make up the complete Mystery Babylon Whore, every soul that does not have its name written in the Lambs Book of Life is listed in the books of Mystery Babylon. Taken over by the Antichrist, called even the eighth kingdom for one hour and is of the seven, namely revised Rome with the ten horns. Like a cage filled with every foul spirit and every unclean and hateful bird on the earth. Notice when the Angel announces in the eighteenth-chapter of Rev. that Babylon is fallen, Babylon is fallen, he has dropped the word, Mystery. I do not believe there is any Mystery left about it at that time. Of course, it never was a mystery to God or God's people that have gotten to know God's Word well.

The whole creation is going to be burned up. There, the Bible starts talking about the new heavens and earth appearing. (Quoting from the Bible) I want to think that every word of this book is taken from the Bible.

If you think we have seen wars and rumors of war, people killing people, and families betraying one another, and all the other things that Jesus talked about. Like the sun being blackened, earthquakes like we've never seen before, rivers turning to blood. All matter of men, small and great, hiding in and calling to the rocks and mountains to fall on them to hide them from the *face of the one on the throne.* The sun scorching men, for a five-month period where men will seek to die but death will flee from them. Jesus pouring out his wrath of torcher on all the earth, pleading with mankind, what is left of them, to repent. But Jesus said they would be blaming him for the plagues, cursing him and would not repent. This must mean the majority representing the whole, for he mentioned some that repented and gave glory to God.

I'm allowed to tell us now, at-this-time we haven't seen anything yet. Wait until the seven-year week of Jesus pouring out his wrath, referred to all up threw the Bible that it is coming. We are nearing times that most of us cannot imagine and no one has seen times like these before, and will never see times like them again. Jesus saying it will be a blessing to die in the Lord, from here on out. If you are already with him at Jerusalem and have not received the Mark is the only safe place to be. And I hope America, that is depending upon us here in America will be safe. Them Muslim Antichrist will cut your head off, and Mystery Babylon will help them. And around sixty-percent of our country belonging to them now.

Jesus said for us to pray that we would be found worthy to stand before him and not go through these things. Sounds mighty much like he is saying that death in Jesus, wherever he is at, would be better than living in these times. Receiving his Spirit would be receiving death to the carnal body that has receive the Mark of a Man. I am convinced that I am standing before Jesus now, every day. Some people think they will require a rapture.

He did name a point in time to John and told him to write it down. He also mentioned a time in the Old Testament where he said God was calling his people home and no one was taking it to heart. But I have never read where I will have to wait on or pray for a rapture. I've said before, it's not that I do not believe there is a rapture, just not one like the big boys are preaching. I suppose it is owing to what one calls a rapture. The word is not one of God's words.

I do not find the word in my Bible, nor one that it replaces, nor one that replaces it. So, it is a carnal word rather than a Spiritual one. I prefer to just leave it alone, rather than try to build one up, a word that would need established by two and three witnesses from God's Word. I do not see that Jesus needed any of my help to write the Bible. I am sure, if he would have needed that word, he would have put it in there when he wrote the Bible.

Man's mind is small, weak, foolish, and flimsy when it is compared to a Spirit, or the Word of God, but try to tell that to a carnal mind. He will probably want to give one a demonstration, free of charge. I have not found a Bible statement to be wrong yet, but have found a lot of statements that was supposed to be from the Bible, but were taken out of context and was not established with two and three witnesses, that was just as false as could be, the way they were being used. The Bible is the Spirit of God in Spiritual Language form. I do believe it is high time for the ones who claim to be Christians to awake and see one can trust the Bible completely, and far, far, over any college professor if one knows how to use it. Paul said so plainly, but words that man has built up I do not care for. Rapture is just one of them.

Like everything else God made, our mind is made with two sides. We have the carnal side and the spiritual side. If Satan is allowed, he will take total control of the carnal side and kill all the spiritual side he possibly can. He is carnal and knows it very well, without the Spirit of God no man is a match for Satan and his imps. He is there for no other reason but to kill, steal and destroy, anything of mankind our God. Satan's spirits are scared to death of Jesus' Spirit. But not of man without him.

Satan never sleeps, in that aspect he is like God and can appear as an angel of light, and sing like a Mocking Bird, he has his own built-in musical instruments. He is seeking whom he may devour. God says he is beautiful, everything about him is to deceive mankind. God referred to him as the god of this world. Given that position by mankind.

It is a never-ending battle, actually, a war with mankind, until

Jesus throws him into the eternal lake of fire along with every soul whose name is not written in the Lamb's book of life. The world seems to be full of high-pressured, fast-talking, pushy-salesmen, trying to put words in your mouth then get you to sign off on them. A Christian has no part with such people. I've never seen a case that I needed one of them to be on my side for me. Satan and his imps must rank around the top of that heap. One sure needs to learn to pick them out. Any preacher that is not preaching Truth is not completely of the Spirit of God. But be careful, God has been known to use Satan himself to deliver his people.

Satan's people, out of ignorance, delivered Jesus to the cross, to the will of God. I have written much in other books, the only way I know one to be able to be sure, is to know the spirit you are dealing with, and the spirit you are dealing from. Too heck with judging the deed, just be with the Spirit of God at the end. That is Jesus Christ in person. He will judge every deed, the Bible says he is busy judging every day, everybody will receive a fair deal.

Experience is a wonderful teacher, but it is usually very expensive and costly. One cannot live long learning by too many mistakes or by experience all time. Better look around and learn by other's mistakes, or read some decent books like the Bible. They do not cost one so much and you will live longer by believing it, might even learn to enjoy life.

God says to try the spirits, you can study your Bible and do that without gambling so many high stakes, like your life. Whether they know it or not, everybody tends to mess with someone else's mind, but only an evil spirit will do it just for his own gain and your loss. Why God uses the word, *mind*, so much in his Word. He even told us we could have the mind of Jesus Christ. As a fact, he recommended it strongly. We will need to fit our mind with it. Not the other way around.

Life itself is somewhat of a gamble, we should learn the Spirit of Truth, it is the only sure-thing in this world that is a sure-thing every time. It pays to get to know the Spirit. If it is the Spirit of God it is a sure-thing; if it is a sure-thing, it is the Spirit of God. If it is not the Spirit, it is just an image. The dictionary says carnal is anything apart from the spirit. God says anything carnal is dead and just an image of the Spirit, including our fleshly bodies.

The (Spirit language; Bible) is the same one God confused from the earth to divide mankind all over the earth. Scattering it worked well but it has served its purpose, God is ready to bring them back together. The ones that are ready to unite with God instead of contrary to God. In other words, the other side and going the other way. Mankind has excepted the carnal language and needs to except and learn the Spiritual Language again.

I do not believe it is out of line to believe the first language that the whole earth spoke, before God confused it from the earth, probably did not make a sound. Something like we call telepathic. But God confused that language from the earth and every creature had to learn to communicate with other like creatures. That not only divided humans, it put a divide between man and animal creatures and creeping things. And to a large degree, between the spirit world and mankind. God said the serpent was subtler than all the others.

Jesus says his Spirit is the life, the truth, the light and everything else a man needs to survive. God divided the world by confusing the one language they had, he will unite them together again by restoring it back to the ones that will hear and believe his one Spiritual Language of the Bible. It is a must to hold them together again and as one with God. This is what I intended this book to be about. A language between man and God, the Mark of the Beast is undoubtable a language but not one I would care to buy into.

Every word should be established with two and three witnesses from God's Word this is a Spiritual Language which we must learn to replace the mind to mind Language that a spirit still speaks until today. Christ says he does not receive a testimony from man, God does not need nor will he receive anything carnal unless it is born again and made new. Every word that is not found in the King James

Authorized Bible is a carnal word, and is to be established from the Bible that Jesus wrote, as truth or as a lie.

Everything is what it is, depending on where you are looking at it from. The carnal and the Spirit are backwards to one another, they see things from opposite sides, and are going in opposite directions. This would explain a lot as to the disagreement between Christians and people of the world, they are not looking at things from the same position. Or better said, from the same Spirit. There is to be no spiritual divisions among God's people. They are all one in the Spirit of God.

One will only understand that, by faith alone. Faith is believing, God is a Spirit and says you cannot please him without faith. Paul called us a new creature if we have received the Spirit of Christ and rejected the flesh. Peter and Jesus called it being born again. Anything else is carnal. I preach hard, the Spirit and mankind lives in two different worlds. Man must make some changes to cross over, and can only do it with the help of the Spirit of God, if you find your life in this world, you have lost the Spirit of God, worth checking into. I'm sorry for people that have it so good in this world and bosting it to be the Spirit of God, NOT.

One needs to know the world he lives in and is aligned with. This world has a different spirit and is lost from the Spirit of God. I hope you have noticed, everything I have been writing is pointing to one thing, we must look to the Spirit of God in these last days. Every day that gets more important from here on out.

I do not object to calling this whole Spiritual World, "An in your mind thing." I believe the Bible calls it the same thing. This is the reason we are told we can have the mind of Christ and many more such things. As I have said the mind and the spirit is the same organ in our body. Even the world has received this fact. Did you ever see the Paul Newman movie "Cool Hand Luke" where Paul Newman could not be shaped to fit in the old southern plantation prison? When the prison guards would punish him they would ask him, "You got your mind right, boy?" "You got your mind, right?"

I have used that story a few times in my forty years of preaching. When I started out preaching I got a few miles of revelations out of that line, "You got your mind right, boy?" God has told us to get our minds right, and Christians should never forget it. God cannot work with a cantankerous spirit, or mind. Even our head-shrinks speak of people with or without a right mind.

Head shrinks are trained to read and understand the spiritual side of man's mind. They don't like to call it that, it sounds too religious for them, implies a weakness below their education level, they think. It was Will Rogers that said, "There is nothing any dumber, than an educated man, out of the field he was educated in." The mind is like everything else God created, it has two sides. The carnal side and the Spiritual side, the carnal side is evil and run by the spirits that were of the one third of God's created beings that rebelled from God and was threw out of heaven by Michael the Arc Angel. Ending up on the earth with mankind, God has had to restrict them ever since.

They are all carnal (Apart from God) and was totally defeated by Christ at the cross. They have been severely restricted since then, they cannot lay a finger on me and you, except temping our minds with temptation of our own lust and ambitions of our own greedy bodies that are much carnal, and desire to run things over God. They will never do that. They have nothing but lies and lying promises for you and me to work with or against.

I have said and believe that anything, no matter how small, can infest and wreck one's entire mind if one allows it to do so. Satan is always trying to do that by setting on our carnal side and trying to kill the Spiritual side of our mind. It only must be allowed to possess it first, to completely control it. Satan is always trying to do just that. God has said he will turn a person over to a reprobate mind to believe a lie and be dammed, if that is what one desires. That is the biggest thing that has happened to this country. God gives us everything we desire and deserve. Seems we desire a reprobate mind.

God will not fight you, if he does, you are an instant looser.

When Satan is controlling one's mind, he is in charge. This is what is known as, Devil possessed. I have stated, in my observations, it seemed I could find more people possessed with *religion*, than perhaps any other one subject. I would not know how to check it out for sure, just an opinion I guess.

A head-shrink is a trained expert in thinking he can handle the spiritual side of mankind. If he does not know, the Spirit like everything else, has distinctly two sides, good and evil, he could be a very dangerous man. Carnal man is always trying to operate on the spiritual side and does not know one thing about it. The man must know enough about the difference in the two worlds to be stable, God says a double minded man is unstable in all his ways. If one has not studied the Bible he would not know much about a double mind.

Religion is a very powerful thing when it comes to handling mankind. The Devil is the most religious thing on earth. He will accept and claim and peddle, any false religion there is, like it will get you to heaven. The same thing from Mystery Babylon. He is not all that hard to please or get along with, just that you cannot get along well with anybody else. Have you ever been told, don't talk politics or religion to a friend? Ever wonder why? I've been told that, perhaps a few dozen times, but I still do not buy it. A person that can't stand my religion is not my friend. Politics is not very far behind. That will solve that problem. You are free to check into it.

Any man that places himself above or between me and my God cannot be my friend. How can Jesus stick closer to you than a brother when a brother insists on standing in between you and God? A many people cannot read their Bible very well and understands it less. And some of them are trying to preach, I pray for them, maybe God can use them some place. Hope their leading to, is greater than their leading away. God has told us to examine and judge ourselves.

I am no judge, but do know the Scriptures very well, and they will tell you about good and evil and am told the scriptures are Jesus Christ himself. He will be the judge, I would not want to get in his way. I hate to think of such a thing. I guess I missed a lot of things, but I was taught if one cannot say something to help a situation, it is probably better to just keep quite unless spoken to or asked something. We are told to pray without ceasing and preach the word to the world. He did not say, only if they like it or pay you well for it.

The Bible is Truth, truth is good, the world is carnal and is evil, evil is a lie. A man that preaches should know the difference. If he doesn't, how does he know what he is preaching? God says to establish every word from the mouth of two or three witnesses and the Bible being the only truth I believe it would be the only place to find the witnesses that a child of God could depend on. God is always right, man is only right when he can be established in truth. We must not only know the truth, we are commanded to live and walk in truth.

This is not as difficult as it sounds, one must believe and love God, he will do the rest, put doubt from your mind. Satan and the world will break all contact with God for you, if you allow them to do it. The flesh must die out, it will lead into shipwreck, so we must meditate on God's Word day and night, resist the temptation of the flesh, putting it out of the mind. This can only be done if one will love and believe God, and trust him. This is when the troublesome burdens and weights will leave one's body giving him the very energy to go on and be established in the right. I believe the word established is the key word in obtaining all these things, you can never do it trying to please both the world and God.

Satan is set with one-third of God's angels that rebelled for no other purpose than to knock you off your feet. Don't even think you can stand if you have not been established in the Spirit of God. Do not get confused in the switching around in so many names. Jesus, the Son of God, the Spirit of God, the Word of God, the Creator, and maybe a few dozen other names, are the same person. The Bible says so, and if you have one you have the others.

Satan is trying to separate them in anybody's mind that he can, and confuse them with any way he can. Why we need to keep reading our Bible and not give any attention to Satan and his lies.

Any time Satan is trying to give you an apple, you can bet it has a worm in it. We must learn the difference between the voice of God and the voice of Satan. If we don't we are living dangerously to say the least and time is getting shorter every day.

The difference in the voices are not so much in the tones of the voices, as in the contents of the message. *Mystery Babylon Whore* is coming up with this *Mark of the Beast* to install in a human body, to make it into a totally machine-controlled-beast. Neither one of these spiritual beast, are known to have the Spirit of Truth, or to tell anything but lies. If one will receive the Spirit of Jesus Christ which cannot receive any part of a lie or be led by it, this will be a guarantee that you will never be given this Mark of the Beast. This will separate the hypocrites and the ones who just think they have the Spirit. From the ones that are established in the Spirit of God.

I've often said there is a lot of people that just have enough religion to be miserable. I do not know where the cut off place is. I believe every man should have one. It should be at the place where it has been discovered. This, is why no man can ever judge another man. God has said for every man to judge himself. I know there is a place we can have enough to stand for ourselves and be sure of it. If you can believe God. God has assured us we will be a tried and proven people. There will be a record kept for the ones who failed, for there is no excuse for failing, for God will carry the ones through that cannot make it on their own. If they will just hold on to him.

It makes no difference if I judge you are not, you can be assured, we will be judged by our creator. It is important to know the Word of God, and to have some close brethren that does, for we are told to look out for one another. Not to order one another around, but to preach and explain the Word. A person that hates to be corrected is more apt to be the one that is wrong. Instead of getting offended, one should learn to be able to explain himself and to convince the gainsayer. You will both learn to grow in the Lord by doing such.

I have been trying to bring this writing up and make a few points and drop a few facts that may be a little hard for some people to follow. Unless one can do a little research and studying. Any statement can be either proved or disapproved in the Bible if it concerns the Spirit or life, if you will learn how to use it.

This is what will establish anyone with God, and settle any disagreement between two level headed people. That rest entirely upon the individual, just how much he can receive, explain and believe the Bible. I maintain that I can establish, any quote in here that I have made, by two or three witnesses from the Bible. Or I will do some heavy apologizing, and some thanking somebody.

I just want it to come from the Bible, it has already judged everything. It is the only thing I know that is always right, and the only thing God will need to use at judgment. We all have more to be thankful for than we like to admit. One can

find that out if he will study the Bible. It is the Language of the Spirit of God, it is Jesus in person. The one and only thing that is nothing but truth, and the whole Truth.

God has said, he will put it in the hearts of the Antichrist Kingdoms to hate the Mystery Babylon Whore. They are to eat her flesh and burn her with fire from the earth. This is not hard to see coming and why. The Antichrist Muslims are built on hating and sworn to kill all Christians from the earth. While the Mystery Babylon Whore will accept any religion on the earth that will accept the Pope as God. They like for the world to refer to them as Christens. They are trying to get together now and we know they are going to come together. God says they will. Since the Bible is Jesus Christ, don't that make it the only True Religion in the earth? Why would anyone want to try and buy a false religion from any other denomination? It is no marvel that there are going to be so many people going to miss the right way, they cannot seem to recognize Truth. It is Christ and the only way, anything else is just a false way and easy found.

If you could count the many denominations you would have some idea of how many false ways there are available. They cannot all of them be right, Jesus said it is a straight and narrow way. It is the other way that is broad and has so many people on it. The two biggest denominations I know of are the Antichrist ten-kingdom Muslims and the Mystery Babylon Whore there at Rome.

How do they think they are going to get them two religions together? No ship has been sent to sail with two captains, at least and came back that way. The secret is they both have the same god (Satan) but hardly know it yet. The Antichrist will war with and defeat the False Prophet and burn her city off the map. Together they will go after the annihilation of the Jews. That will place them against Jesus Christ and will bring about their end. The Antichrist and False Prophet being cast into the lake of fire that burns forever and ever. The Devil being locked up with a seal of darkness and put into the pit for one thousand years. You can read all about it in the Bible. Talk about a good book?!

Jesus will release him after the thousand-year reign, for the soul purpose for Satan to go into all nations of the earth to persuade every soul that has not been happy with the righteous thousand-year rule of Jesus Christ, to join him in a campaign to surround and kill Jesus with his little camp of saints there at Armageddon. Satan will convince them that it will be easy having the largest army ever been formed on the earth following him.

This is referred to as the battle of the great day of God Almighty. At the end Jesus will toss the Devil, and Mystery Babylon with every soul that has not its name written in the Lamb's Book of Life into the fire that burns for ever and ever, where the Antichrist and the False Prophet already are. The ones whose names are not in the Lambs Book of Life will be listed in the Mystery Babylon's False Prophet's books. Whether they know it are not.

God keeps many books. Not that he needs them, just to show them to us, I guess. He will have the records right there. When he judges the world and every person, and gives each person their reward, good or bad. I cannot figure the sequence in all of this, I believe God meant for us not to be able to, but I know it will come to pass.

Then the new heavens and earth are seen coming down from Heaven.

A FEW WORDS ABOUT RELIGION

Religion, may be the most powerful thing to man on the earth, every man has his own. Has been much that way since creation when God gave man the garden. I have written much on how God has made most everything in twos, religion is no different. There is the true religion, which is the Spirit of Christ, the Truth. And there is the Antichrist religion which is nothing but a lie from the ground up. But Satan will buy and peddle any and every false religion that comes by, that is his business. True and false have been battling each other since the creation, probably before, and will be battling one another every day as long, as time, as we know it, does exist.

The Bible has recorded the history of man, from the beginning in the garden, to the last day that time will exist. We can read all about it in the Bible, seems kind of amazing to me. For there is not a false statement in it, nor a word left out of it, even though we will not fully understand it without help from the Spirit of God. The Bible says so. The Bible is the Spirit of God and record of man from the beginning to the end, but says very little about God himself before or after mankind, it would have very little to do with our salvation. But promises no word in it will fail until all be fulfilled. There, is where faith must come in.

When you are reading the Bible, you are reading God's judgement on everything. Dealt to every person the same way. I have written in other books, and maybe this one, about how everything is what it is, depending on where one is looking at it from, and how the Spirit and the carnal are looking at everything from the opposite side from one another. They just about see nothing alike, why we must always look at things from God's point of view.

The Spirit of God is always seeing things correctly. The Spirit of God should be in everybody while bringing them all together in one, for the betterment of every person. Together we can pull a big load easier. Pulling against each other, we can move nothing. It would be a glorious sight if we could all hear and believe everything in Truth, which is Jesus Christ. The world could not withstand us. God is the Truth, anything contrary to him is carnal and a lie, and will never make it into the Spirit of God. This can only be seen and done, in and by, the Spirit, which is The Word of God. In the Spiritual Language of God.

I know this is hard for a carnal man to appreciate and I can tell you why. Man is very likely to ask, "What's in this for me?" when he has been offered any deal. The writing is about nothing for sale but a secure future in the hereafter promised all through the Word of God and does not promise anything "To me" past eternal life.

Mankind is so selfish and carnal, he cannot completely fit with another man, only in the Spirit. This leaves out all mankind if his flesh cannot die out. How many men do you know that is agreeable to that? I am me, and you are you, we can become one only in the Spirit, it is the only thing that can tolerate us both.

Religion, is simply what a person believes in and what he looks towards to put his trust into for eternity, two choices. Christ or the world. It might not be so important if it was not so permanent, like forever. But it is, the most permanent thing you will ever face in this life. We go through life making choices, every choice we make, we will live and die with.

God says we will give account for every idle word. This does not necessary mean one will be judged for every word one utters, but he will be accountable for every word he says by the way he said it, for the rest of his life, if he does not repent. This is the reason we must be going through life repenting for we would never make it otherwise. Repentance comes from the heart, God looks nowhere else for it. He knows the very thoughts and intents of the heart of everyone. Can you explain that to a carnal mind? A carnal mind cannot reach around it. Ever hear anyone ask, got your mind right, boy? We can have the mind of Christ.

We serve God by faith, faith is believing. A carnal man cannot believe it, so he cannot have it. Sounds to me like that kind-of leaves the carnal man out. When I came to be reading these things in the Bible, I got interested in checking out a little bit of what God considers carnal to be. I consulted my dictionary to see what it said, it said no more or less than this, carnal is, "Anything apart from the spirit." No wonder God talked so much about it. I hardly know of any plainer or bigger word than that. It kind of underlined all my preaching of how important the Spirit is, and how needful it is to get to knowing something about it. God is the Spirit, anything apart from him is carnal or dead.

Then comes the importance of how lost and helpless we are without the Spirit. Enough to get a sober man to thinking. God said to establish every word with two or three witnesses. I have figured out that is talking about both ends of the word. Where it came from and where it is going, by the way it is used. If one becomes that well informed I promise one will have fewer discussions about the Bible and less people trying to instruct him. They will more than apt want to hear from him. If they care about their soul. Some just do not believe and rather not hear you talk about it. That is one of each man's choices and all men's problem, he will live and die with his choices.

Now, I do not know if that is good or bad in every case, but know it is an automatically sure thing. People have a dread and sometimes a dislike for the plain truth, when they have been feeding on a lie and their flesh enjoying it. The Bible will expose and condemn all lies if you can quote and establish the Bible correctly. These things underline my, kind-of, dislike for denominations. I know their answers for being wrong, "Oh but nobody can be perfect all the time."

Jesus Christ, was and is, the Bible is perfect and says so. If the person is trying to cut me down and put me in my place or justify himself, he is very wrong, for I am not talking about me, but the Bible and Truth. It is the only thing that can justify anything. It is not wrong, nowhere in it. If I am misquoting it, that is another horse and of a different color. But like I was saying there is a way of establishing every word with the Bible, or God would not have told us to do it. But he did, and told us how. How many people do you see that knows that? Or better yet, how many do you see that does it?

Jesus Christ is truth, no part of a lie in him, carnal is nothing but a lie. True religion is nothing but truth and God's Word. So, true religion will accept no part of a lie but only truth, while carnal accepts any religion on the earth *but* truth, telling all people it will save their soul while promising them everything they want here and in the hereafter. Where is Satan or any man going to come up with life and heaven for all his people on this earth? He was cast out of heaven; his lies are innumerable and sound so good the world wants to believe them and the world can do as it pleases. Adam and Eve gave it to Satan. Every person either believes and is led by the Spirit of God or he belongs to Satan. I cannot change that story.

I do not want seventy-two virgins and all the dope in the world when I get to heaven. Any man that will fall for that does not have a sound mind and he will never find such a heaven as that. Anybody that buys that should be able to see, he is only looking for self as his God, with a god that is his servant. There is no such god. With Jesus Christ, I do not plan to be apart from the Spirit. Jesus is the Spirit and our only hope on this earth. That will not bring you many compliments, so my writings will not impress the world.

John said, if every word was written that should be written about Jesus Christ, he reckoned the books of the world could not contain them. I fully believe there is not a wrong word, over exaggerated word, or one word used, in the Bible that is not supposed to be in the Bible. That means I believe every word that is written in the King James Authorized Translation. Jesus said he wrote it, and it is him. We are told to preach it to every creature in the earth. That includes every word that is in it now, and forever. God never changes. Are you looking for a writer that can offer you more, I am not he?

If man adds or changes one word in it, it cannot Spiritually, or legally, be called the King James Authorized Bible. The Bibles that have been changed and rewritten must be labeled by the name of the ones that wrote them or at least authorized them. They will be responsible for their work. It will be counted among the books of the world, even if some of them are mighty good books. Jesus did not write them, or at least did not say he did. He claims the original King James and tells when, where, how and why, he did it, around sixteen-hundred AD. In all other writings, that is, or has been, I have not read where Jesus claimed writing a word of them. The Bible is the only Spiritually written book on this earth. It makes up the Spiritual Language of the earth. The Bible does not stand for all the English Language, just the words used in it. That is why Jesus says if one word of it is changed, it is not me.

I have not even heard of a book or any writings that can even start to equal or claim the honorary standings or credits that is accredited to the King James Translated Bible. It stands in an honor all by itself. Several millions of people have died protecting it from Satan's false religions in the world in just these last one thousand years, it has been written by King James' Authorization.

The Devil has hated it more than Jesus Christ himself. He thought he killed Jesus.

But he just woke up his influence, he lost that battle very greatly.

I am forced to believe that all *other* writings in the world must be called carnal writings, while the entire King James contains, only and all, the Spiritual Writings that is on, or has been on, this earth. Not all the writings about the Spirit, but all the writings of the Spirit. I do not know of another power that can touch its shadow, or can even get close enough to see it. It takes the Spirit of God.

This should give any Christian a window to see why the Bible, is and should be, such a cherished and Holy Book. Jesus said, it was the way, the truth, the life, the light, the Spirit, and everything else that is right and positive. Even said it was him. One can only see that with the Spirit of God, and some of our largest denominations does not even believe in the Spirit of God. What do they believe in beside what they already have? Who is going to resurrect them, their father? Here on the Earth? They sure do not have a computer that can resurrect anybody. If someone in the world is trying to reason a rewritten Bible and a corrected one to you, ask him when did Jesus tell anyone he was going to need himself corrected, or updated? He is the Spirit, he can start in where the computer leaves off.

What I am trying to say is, every word that is in the King James Bible is a Spiritual Word. It has the power of the Spirit with it, when used properly. Any word that is not in the King James Bible is a carnal word and will need to be able to be established by two and three places in the Bible as to how it is used or it cannot be considered as a Gospel Word.

I am not really moved by a carnally preached sermon. I will try to get as much out of it as I can, but will be measuring every word of it from the Bible, it is the judge, it has already judged the world and everything in it. When you read it, you are reading God's judgment on anything it is about, for it is what God is going to use on Judgment day. It will not have one word changed in it, what it means today is what it will mean on judgment day. What it will mean on judgment day is what it means today. Why argue about the scriptures, just establish each word as God commanded us to do and accept it? No person is anointed above you other than to preach the gospel, it is up to you to receive it for yourself, not him to measure you.

Too many people want to hold onto the world with one hand and the Lord with the other. I do not know if they will make it or not, but I do know, if one knows God, he will be one miserable person until he gets it right with God or at least thinks he has. And will seldom be a person that lives to be an old man if he chooses to live his life battling with the Spirit of the Lord. It is always right and not known for giving much quarters to anything that is wrong. Wrong is out of God's territory. We are to seek God, not command or instruct him.

You ask him about things, you don't tell him anything. There is nothing he don't know. If his chosen cannot take orders, they will not be giving any from God. Satan has a lot of people thinking they are in charge, but they are only in charge of the Devil's people not of them that are of God. You can take that to the bank, if you are not bankrupted, they will cash it for you.

I am hoping to build this writing up to a few points, or *facts,* that I can drop and will be understood to the reader as I am meaning to use them. I am fully convinced that any word you can find in the Bible is a Spiritual word. Any word you cannot find in the Bible is a carnal word. Since God confused the one whole language that the earth used, to divide up the people at the tower of Babel, an ordinary man knew not one word of Spiritual Language, and had very little of God in him but the fear. Until Jesus came. Maybe Daniel, Elijah, Solomon and a very few others, but I hardly call them ordinary men.

Jesus the Spirit, was not given to man until around the year of 00 on our calendar. I do not know a person who knows exactly when that was except on the calendar. I have never saw it there. God spoke in his book to the Hebrews saying, "God, who at sundry times and in diver's manners spoke in time past unto the fathers by the prophets, hath in these last days spoken unto us by his Son." This is where the New Testament comes in at.

Until Jesus came and paid the price for mankind, and sent back the Spirit of God unto all mankind, we had very little of anything of God except his word spoken through his prophets, kings, and judges. Jesus Christ had not been given to man. If you will look very close at the Bible and history, man had a deep inborn fear of God, that he does not have today, he blasphemes, mocks, and laughs at

God with no fear at all. God did not put up with that before Christ came.

God said them that have no God at all, will think more of their god than the ones that have a living God that loves them. God did not put up with any of that before Jesus became the mediator between man and God, the prophets, could not do it. Man would not accept another man, and no man could live long enough to carry it on. God is love and them that know him loves his Son, them that know Jesus loves and trust God. They come together. There are not words to make us understand how much Jesus paid for God's Word to stay alive until he got his harvest picked from this world.

Jesus gave us so much, and it seems instead of us giving him the love and thanks he deserves, we are giving him ridicule and mockery. It will get worse and worse until Jesus will be forced to burn clean, all the evidence of all mankind that would not receive him, that ever existed. Leaving only the smoke of their torment and keeping the few that he accepted for the Father. I know of no one that knows what the smoke will look like. Maybe it will be a little coloration around a small spot like a cloud, just a guess. The clouds are out there in the atmosphere all time if you are seeing them or not. I am sure it will look like torment. As I wrote in one of my other books, "God will have the last laugh."

God has mentioned in his Word, he will laugh at the foolishness of man. He has told us to wise-up, and how to do it, no need for man to stay that way. It is his choice.

I cannot say any more than the Word of God says about this, but I know most people have a question in their mind about the burning up the earth and all the elements thereof. But before I make another comment on anything, I want you to know God can do anything he pleases and any way he chooses. He is going to do everything he says he is going to do. He doesn't need to have my opinion on nothing. There is a lot of room for God to operate in when it comes to making everything new. Like he said he was going to do.

When I was born again I was made into a new creature, but I

look entirely like the same body to the carnal. When God makes all things new, when he returns, like he promised just as he was leaving, all carnal will be gone. I am not going to argue with him about one thing, it will be alright with me, I promise you. Do you think you can trust your neighbor to make all things new, rather than the creator? I believe I rather stay with Jesus. I have seen many things that my neighbors have made. They don't seem to have an eternal look about them.

I've heard them promise many things that was obvious they could not do. I have faith in Christ.

A LITTLE ABOUT WORDS

The deep subject in this writing here in the past few pages, has been on words, written and spoken. Again, Jesus said, "By thy words thou shall be justified, and by thy words thou shall be condemned." Man, that speaks a word that is not a Word of God, is his word, and he will be judged by it. Much more Jesus said about words, his words, God's words, our words, even about the Devil's words. Words are very important, they are the seed and the foundation for the world's communication with one another, and with God. They are like tracks; each man leaves his own. Paul said he spoke no words that did not come from Jesus Christ, and he did not speak carnally. And I do not believe he stuttered either. Every word one speaks is a seed sowed.

God pulled the one language from the earth that the whole earth spoke when they were coming together as one against God at Babel. God wanted them to come together as one but did not want them forming against him. I do not believe he was worried about man taking his seat over, like man is always trying to do. Just that in the end not one soul would be saved. So, he confused their language, or words. Scattered them over the whole earth and each group had to develop their own language to communicate together, and seek God the same way. The confusion has lasted until today. God has put us a one Spiritual Language back together again. Look for it to be identified and explained in this book. Called the Spiritual Language of God.

As man has been overall maturing, them that have not been completely turned away from God have been given Jesus Christ in Spiritual Word form. Peter and the other disciples opened the Kingdom of God in one Spiritual Language again at Pentecost. Spoken in the Spirit and every person that was there understood them in his own language. One of the more significant and greatest happenings between God and man, the pouring out of Jesus Christ upon all mankind.

Speaking in tongues is a great and rare gift of God and very helpful if understood, and used properly, it is not for the believer, but for the unbeliever. It is not given to impress people and make one look superior to everyone else. Or to take charge of a praise service. Paul said if there was no interpretation to not let it interrupt the service, and then limit it to a reasonable amount. Pray for an interpreter, tongues and an interpretation, equal a prophesy. It is a very legitimate gift of the Spirit but I believe I have seen it kind-of abused, or misused, along with several other gifts. But I would not dare rebuke it. It is from the Spirit of God, unless somebody is trying to fool around. That is dangerous.

The Spirit needs to be sought after and studied and understood, but never ignored. No one needs to depend entirely upon someone else's spirit, each person should have his own experience with the Spirit of God. Work to insure one's own salvation. Jesus has become our complete soul, language, Spirit, and everything else we need, if we can just love, trust, and believe him and be born again into his Spiritual Word. This is the way it is taught in God's Word. It teaches we can do nothing without it. Of course, this is talking in and from the Spirit world, and can only be understood there, but still true.

The Bible calls them a *new creature,* we must die out to the flesh with its carnal ways. Carnality cannot have it, for carnal insist on having complete control of itself. That does not include Jesus Christ and there is no other way to God than through him. No fleshly man can take his place only as his servant, and serve him. He will only save us when we come to the place where we admit we can do nothing without him, and he is a Spirit. The carnal cannot see, believe, or tell that story.

I am not asking you to judge anybody, but God has told us to know them that are in the Spirit of God, to mark them that are not, and be unto them as a heathen. If there come any unto you and bring not this doctrine, receive him not into your house. Neither bid him God speed. If you do you will be partaker of his evil deeds. But what do you hear the ungodly hypocrites preaching to us from everywhere?

Does a few of this sound familiar? *We must love and embrace everybody and everything, if they ask anything of you, you must give it to them, and you must bless and support their evil deeds, you must tolerate and ignore everything or you are judging. You cannot offend another person's religion. Which says, you act like I act or you do not know God.* I could fill a few pages of false doctrine here but surely that is enough to get somebody to looking at what the Bible actual says at least a little bit. Not one of them false statements I just quoted came from the Word of God. They came from Satan. You can learn many more amazing things. If you would learn from your Bible, not from false teachers. God warned us they would be numerous in the last days.

I have heard enough preaching coming from ungodly preachers that cannot read their Bible, to do me a lifetime. All of them are not coming from the pulpit. They do not know that God said we are to be able to establish ever Word of God with two and three witnesses before it can be called the Truth or Gospel. I have heard, mostly from the world, preaching to us we must accept queers, same sex marriages, child molesters and anything they can think of. Telling us how unholy and hypocritical we are if we are not doing these things. If I find any such junk as that in my Bible I will throw it away for I know it will be a wrong book. I have had better raising than that. God said, if a man come to you preaching any other doctrine beside Christ and he crucified, do not let him into your house.

There is no such thing as one place in the Bible calling another place a lie. If they are thinking that, then somebody does not know how to read the Bible, they better find themselves a man of God to help them. I would make sure he believes in the Spirit of God. I can hardly imagine true religion that don't, but they are plentiful that think differently. I guess somebody else is carrying their religion for them. That would include, faith, Spirit, Christ, power, anything else God promised to his people.

In around sixteen-hundred A D, England was getting so confused and mixed up and divided by so many different religions, they were not holding to God's one Spiritual Language. Even though they were holding on to God as best they could, every denomination thought they were the one that was right. Mystery Babylon and Christians killing each other constantly. They were lost without a light. As far as I know Mystery Babylon does not accept a Bible, just a pope, called in the Bible, "The False Prophet." This is the light that was lost, the Word of God. Anyone that has not excepted it today, is still lost.

Mystery Babylon, raised up at Rome, pretending to be the vicar of Christ and the only true religion but not believing in the Spirit of God or a new birth. And they were going to rule the world by killing everybody that did not accept their religion. Teaching what they say was the only gospel and they were the only one that could say what it meant. I reckon they thought you needed to be born into their spirit. I will not lay my soul and the souls of my family, friends, and church, into somebody else's hands, and depend on someone else to carry them for me. God has said he gave my family to me and I am held responsible for them and I would answer to him for them. No place have I read where he named a religion that I could trust that unto, that could take my responsibility from me, less than the Spirit of God.

Where did they need Christ? Seems they had everything covered themselves. I believe they think so too. They had killed well over one hundred million people, burning most of them at the steak and beheading them with a guillotine, whole families at a time and whole villages by pushing them over a cliff and many other ways, God's people was growing more oppressed and fewer by the day. Before America, put them down twice with two world wars, with Christ's help. America became a thorn in their side, slowed them up a bit. Until we let them take us over through our schools, just like they told us they would do. (Speaking of being deaf and blind) that should give you a perfect example.

But like the Jews coming out of Egypt, they would not completely kill off the people that God told them to kill. If God's people would have obeyed him from the beginning we would be running the world today instead of Satan's people. We would be living in a world that God could tolerate and bless. God will not tolerate a world for very long, where man is insisting on being his own God with the biggest one being the ruler and trying to rule the world. Jesus says, that is *his* Job. The hypocrites telling God he is wrong, when God says the inhabitants of the world is nothing to him. Are you going to judge him? You have probably gotten him scared to death. sic

God got so tired of delivering them over and over from people he had told them to kill, their women, their old, their young, their animals, everything that breathed, but they would not do it. Only killing the ones that would not let them be their God. Until he finally told them, "You are killing the ones I do not want killed, you keep alive the ones I want you to kill, and now I am not going to let you kill them." "I will set them around you for a thorn in your side and when you will not obey me, I will turn them loose on you a little at a time until you do."

God said that, over four-thousand years ago. Can you not see it today? God has worked much that way ever since. God has told us the day will come when there will not be any left to turn them loose on, except the Jewish nation. The world will show God they had rather die than repent. In fewer words, God was saying to them, I will be God over my creation, like it or not. Even if I only have a few remaining. I will turn back to the Jews and come down, save them, set up among them to protect them, let them rule the world with me and the Gentiles I have saved with them. Jesus states that, in the twenty-fourth chapter of Matthew.

So, if you are a saved Gentile better be prepared to go back to the Jews with Jesus. They will be tried, tested and proven, so will you. There will always be consequences when we will not obey God and obey false teachers that actual believe they know what God meant to say, better than he does. If one would establish every word with at least two and three witnesses like God told us, six places in the Bible, to do, and obey God. It would keep that one from being led and confused in every direction one can point. God has said for us to not plant our roots in this world. If we find our life here, we will lose it over there.

God and his people calls that lost. We know he was talking about witnesses coming from God's Word, for Jesus said he does not need or will not receive the witness of man. I learned early, if one puts his trust in a man, and completely followers him, he will fail, no matter how good he is if he is not Jesus Christ. Look around you, I have never seen it not fail. We must learn to keep our eyes upon Jesus Christ.

It has been somewhat that way from the beginning, with God sending them prophets, seers, judges, and kings, teachers, still Israel would not obey him. He warned he would turn them over to Satan if that was what they wanted. It seems that man cannot be left alone to rule himself without totally killing and destroying one another from the earth. This is all that Satan is trying to do, his only purpose, whose side are we on? This should tell anyone why God was forced to accept so few of mankind. Only them that would accept death to the flesh and world. He sent his son to pay the price for every person that would love and accept him, they would have eternal life with him, but the rest will perish.

Would you want God to accept them that are killing his people here, burning them alive at the stake and cutting their heads of, burying them alive? Putting them in jail for saying the name of his Son in public. Do you think he should take them to heaven to live with us forever? We are proving every day, here on earth, we cannot handle them Christ haters. They think they are God's executioners and killing for their god. They are preaching to us here in America, teaching in our colleges (They have freedom of religion you know, along with authority to shut our religion down) why not? They have sworn to rid us from the earth and we elect them for our judges and president, lawyers and school teachers. We don't seem to realize that the Spirit of God is the only real protection we have from them.

They are making our laws, from Washington DC, down to the dog catchers. Teaching our children from colleges down to kindergarten. Making up and approving all our curriculum to our schools, changing our history, teaching our children they are God, and their parents are fools. We told them to bring them up any way they wanted to, we will fire any teacher that speaks out against them. We vote for them every election while eating up their lies. Who do you think is at fault? Blame it on God, that is what God said we would do. Anyone that goes around believing lies is not lead by the Spirit of God.

I remember when I was just a small child almost seventy years ago. I was talking to a very young Muslim person about religion, we identified what we had been raised as. He looked at me with a good-natured smile and said, I will have to kill you one day. I did not think much of it then, and even less of it today. How dumb and vulnerable can one group get? Now we are electing them to run our entire government, and they are still telling us the same thing. I find it hard to believe.

We get threw in jail, if not killed, for mentioning the name Jesus in public or in front of an atheist's kid, or carrying a Bible on government property. When did Christian Americans give up their freedom of religion? When Mystery Babylon taught it out the door, and made us like it. --And doing away with our freedom of speech. How much good is your religion when you cannot speak about it or teach your own family? I was not a full fledge Christian until I was in my thirties, but I was raised better than to believe such obvious lies as that kind of teaching.

God, in talking to his children, said plainly there is a time to kill. What better time do you think he was talking about, than when they are killing, in public, any Christian that they can catch and bragging that they will do it until the last one is gone. How much more asleep can God's people get? And to think most of the so-called Christians are voting for them. I don't think so, calling themselves Christians does not make them one.

They tell us that "*is*" our freedom of religion, and we kiss their toes and thank them for being so gracious to us for not cutting our heads off and allowing us to accept them as our God. Our children cannot say the name Jesus in our public schools. Do you think a Christian would make and enforce such laws for our country? I find it unbelievable how stupid some of my own belief are. I do not believe they are Christians, them that are believing lies and lying to us, preaching such nonsense that it is coming from God. It is not coming from my God.

As I say so often, "I do not see our Christians." Jesus, called us an army, but I cannot see why. We sure do not believe in fighting any more, except with one another. And voting for Muslim's to run our armies while telling us they are going to kill us and raise their flag over Washington DC, using our army and money to help them do it. I wish I could say I was lying or exaggerating, but I see no way I can and be honest and make different statements than that to anybody. Jesus said he was the way, are they carrying him hid somewhere? Is that why we are following them?

We elect the Devil's people to run our country and our army's and teach our Children, so we will not have to fight them, they tell us fighting is contrary to our God's teaching. This is their God's teaching, so we just need to shut-up and obey them, is what they tell us. I have been saying for around forty years now, I believe the people of this world have gone stark-raving mad, and now I am confident Mystery Babylon and the Antichrist has America in tow. We think they are God, I reckon, and we are his favorite people. I believe I had more sense than that when I was born.

God's Word says what he is going to do with them. He is raising up ten antichrist kingdoms in the East, and putting it in their hearts to hate the Babylon Whore. They are going to fake giving their power to the Great Whore but will take them over and eat their flesh and burn their city off the earth. They are trying to join up now. Since they will not read their Bible, they have no clue.

If God is taking them, mad, God-hating, throat-cutting, burning-people-alive-bunch to heaven, he can just leave me with the bunch that will be hiding in the rocks and praying for the rocks to fall on them to hide them from the one that is sitting on the throne pouring out the wrath of God on the world. I believe that is going to be the "Mystery Babylon's" people ruled by the False Prophet from Rome, hiding in the rocks, praying for death. God said he would send an angel flying over them warning his people to get out from among them and receive not of their plagues. Most of them will take the mark of the beast. The ten Antichrist kingdoms are rising now in the Middle East, and are going to give their power to Mystery Babylon, that excepts any false religion that will except their pope for God. They should know that is not going to happen to the Muslims.

The ones that will be giving the Mark of the Beast, that was built by American scientist, and money. The Antichrist will eat their flesh and burn their city off the earth. (Start in the Sixth chapter of Rev. to read the whole story). They will not want to face Christ, on the throne. And for five months they will not be able to die. I am tired of taking orders from such ungodly people, that has us scared to death. Someone just call for arms if you think I won't fight.

Think God, I know he is not going to take them to heaven, without them becoming newly reborn into his Spiritual people. I have often said, if I get to heaven and see Hitler there, I am not going to worry, I know that it is not the same one that was here. He will be born again into the Spirit and made new. (But I would be a little surprised). I do not expect to see him there.

Anybody that can build a building and hire a preacher can start his own denomination, and run it as long, as he has or can get, the money. Just don't call on Jesus too loud or offend a Muslim, you will be arrested. Or Democrat Attorney General, under Obama told us these words. The great Democrat Attorney General for Obama. I can about get sick to look at either one of them. And to think they are Christians? I don't think so.

I do not see how anybody with a right mind can think that might be the correct way God, or our Constitution, or Bible, has instructed us to serve God and our country. And let them teach our children? That is just about the final straw.

Them people do not know the same God that I know, their church is not run by the Spirit of God. Somebody must be praying and seeking God, or God is not in it. If the Spirit of God is running a church and having his way it will be growing with converts. Not in Devil possessed victims. Of course, I am aware of how hard it is to have a prosperous church in this disinterested world today. But to compromise the preaching, and start preaching their lies for them, to me is not the answer. Their hatred is just about got another Civil War started, and I don't believe their anymore ready for it than the last time they started one, but they are determined to have it.

Back to my story about words, England was getting so confused and divided, like America is today. I believe we are worse off today than England ever was, of course I am talking Spiritually and financially. At least they could see they were getting off track and all they needed was an authentic Spiritual Word of God to lead them into unity, and back to God. We are getting worse every day, and apparently don't know it, but in a state of denial. That makes about as bad as one can get.

We have the Word of God (The Bible, Jesus himself) but do not believe it, or believe in fighting to keep it any longer. Teaching our kids, it is evil and a lie. This is not a nation with God running it anymore. Our forefathers of this country, fought the world to build the foundation of this country. Their children, our fathers, fought the greatest, strongest nation in the world so we could have freedom to worship as we pleased, defeated them before we were half grown, won two world wars to keep it. And defeated every other nation that dared to cross us, and our God. I do not believe they read the commandment, "Thou shalt not kill" the same way as they demand it of us today." How many ways can you translate the word kill and confirm it the way it is used with two or three witnesses in the Word of God?

God blessed us to the greatest nation that is, or ever has been, on the face of the earth. Now Mystery Babylon and the rising Antichrist kingdoms have made us ashamed of our God, we are denying and apologizing for him all over the world, and looking at a twenty trillion-dollar debt, and a lost generation of youth that don't know if they are male or female or what they want to marry, a woman or a man, or a horse. And have neither the fear or respect from any nation. Killing one another until it is not safe to walk down the streets.

Killed tens and multi-of tens of millions of unborn and infant babies. Making it a sport to kill anyone in authority. What else have we got to lose? I will tell you, our lives and souls. Tell me again about the word kill. *God said there was a time for us to kill, and a time for us to make alive.* Is your god guilty of teaching us their kind of killing? That is not the God I serve. What part of that can they not hear.

I know again some of the questions you will ask. Are we supposed to give God's blessings and our goods to people that are living like that? It seems to be about all of them. The answer to that is NO. If you will read that order again, there is a time to kill and a time make alive. You should know the differences in the times and who is what. And which one we owe to either one. If we would let the killers kill one another, but seek out the innocent and the ones that need our protection and care to help them as much as we can, I am sure we could help the problem much, and might even eventually eliminate it. If one could find enough Christians. There is where our problem is. They are hard to find.

Now we elect the Devil's people to run our country for we refuse the responsibility. They tell us we are not a Christian nation anymore, that made us glad, now we will not have to fight them, for they are only after the Christians. And for free things they will let us join them if we will not disagree with them, that is what they tell us our God says for us to do. After all Mystery Babylon is running our government, Washington DC, our schools, and teaching our children that government is God and they are the government, and putting them in jail for speaking the name of Jesus Christ. They or running our schools today from our colleges down to kindergarten, teaching them the government is the only God. I do not read that in my Bible, it is why they have been trying to do away with our Bible, or Jesus, for two-thousand years.

How long is God going to tolerate us? He has long since quit blessing us. Our children are gone, we have refused responsibility for them. This is the problem of this country. That is the reason I say this people make me sick. Some of the things the news media and the politicians can come up with, for the cause and the care for our problems.

They seem to think more tax money will fix them all. Makes me want to just get some of them by the shirt collar and slap some sense into them. Instead of working to fix our problems, they spend all their time and our money to blame it on their opponent when it is as plain as day it is them that that are the problem. Our voters are so ignorant, enough to make a grown man cry.

Jesus is not causing our country's problems, and it is not his people causing them. If we had been raising our children up in the fear and admonition of the Lord, like our Bible said for us to do and like our forefathers started out doing in this country. We would have a different people running our country today, and many of our judges and politicians would have been gassed, or hung by now. And we would not be looking another Civil War in the face while they are already blaming it on us. We need to get some Conservative Republicans up there to help Trump instead of the lying, money, stealing Democrats and scared to death stupid Republicans that we have now. I am hoping that these next few elections will wake a few of these people up to see that God's people are not dead like they are hoping for us to be, and trying to accomplish it. We haven't yet begun to fight.

Even fox news was bashing our president for talking a little about our western values in his speech while meeting with Russia's prime minister, Putin, at the G 20 summit in Germany. Their remarks were sounding like Trump was so uneducated and inexperienced in world affairs, as to sound like a high school child talking on such cheap stuff in front of Putin that is so much more sophisticated than Trump. I wonder where did they received their education on values? It is their knowledge, or lack of it, on values, is why this country is on the bottom of the heap of hell-level countries in this world today. Do you think that Democrats can fix it? They stole and spent ten-trillion dollars in the past eight years and only filled their pockets and doubled our debt. The biggest national debt our country has ever seen. I do not feel one bit better off.

Seems to me like I hear the word Democrat mentioned regularly in the Anti-God side. Isn't that the same word I read about in our history, that is now being rewrote, and perverted? The Democrats that rebelled and started the Civil War and almost wrecked the union of the greatest nation ever built? Killed one of our best presidents ever. Building and running the KKK and lynching the republicans. Losing the Korean war, the Vietnam war, teaching our kids that the Christians did it. Trying to make Bush lose ever war he was in, making it cost and dragging it out as much as they could. Setting China and Russia up above us in nuclear weapons and technology, apologizing to the world because we have better service branches and better service men than them.

Because we fear God and do not fear the Democrat, God haters, even though they made America into one of the most indebted nation on the globe. And hanging Republicans from white robes and hoods. I am sure the Lord is going to say, "You knew better." It seems that anybody with eyes should see that the Liberal Democrat dominated cities and states and areas are the ones that are about ate up with natural disasters, God promised that, you know. They don't seem to mind as that is Mystery Babylon's purpose for this country.

We should have been arresting and throwing into jail a few of our movie makers and Holly Wood actors and college professors, and politicians and news reporters, that was selling everything we owned for the money to stay in power, instead of our preachers and parents. I believe we would be looking at an entirely different country and one that could be feeding the entire world and living in safety again. And going fishing two or three days a week. A country that God could bless. If we would just put God back at the head of us again. God said we could do all them things. And we would not owe another country a dime and would not grow hungry and would be able to help other of God's people with God's help. (Not them that worship false gods) If we would just let the Lord be God. Is the only duty he has appointed to us? And stand up for our God that is protecting and providing for our country, and every individual.

God has about run out of patience with us and about ready to tell us we can worship the government, and take their Mark of the Beast and die. Don't worry about nothing, just tell God it is all his fault, blame him. Is what he said we will be doing. Saying, God did not Kill off the Antichrist and the Mystery Babylon Whore for us and they are just too big for us to handle. When we cannot handle our own children? God may say, *"When did you try? Do we think we could live worse than them, blaspheme God, spit in his face and be able to handle Satan's world without Christ?"* Did we think the Devil would fear us and feed us, if we just bow to him? What *are* we thinking? God has warned us as plain as a man can speak. Why do you think Mystery Babylon of Rome has threw the Bible out of our schools while we are sleeping at their feet? They are obviously smarter than we are.

If the Christians would fight the Antichrist, Mystery Babylon and their people half as hard as we fight one another, we would be running the world today with God instead of Satan. It was God's plan for us to do that. God has said, in the last days the Antichrist would wear God's people out and he would be given power over them and to put them to death. It is looking like we are doing that for him, reckon that might make us the Antichrist's people? We are doing his job for him.

God has expressed plainly it is the one that has Christ that has the power. Power is what the world respects most. We can either walk with Christ, which is all power, or walk without him and have the power our own two hands can muster up as long, as it will last. Before we start asking why this and why that. Man must remember there is no place in the Bible where Jesus ever gave in to temptation to try and impress man or to prove anything to him by any force.

If he did he would be busy day and night trying to convince man. Man would be running him, not him running the earth. That will never happen, but God has said we will reap what we sow.

How can one think Jesus is so naïve, when he is the giver of all knowledge? Our whole life is laid out already, we just have the choice to walk in it, aligning with Christ or suffering the *consequences*, they are both laid out plain. The New Testament is full of people trying to temp Christ to come on their level and prove himself to them. If they want to believe him they will, if not, they won't.

About forty years ago I was new in Christ and reading my Bible almost constantly. I read that about Satan being given power over us and to put us to death. It bothered me, I did not understand. I set into prayerfully studying my Bible and I guess giving God a terrible time over seeing that. I learned many things about my Bible with all my studying for several months but did not get my answer to why God was giving Satan all that power over us. I had about given up on getting an answer. When in one of the services we were called on for routine prayer, I just turned around, knelt on my seat and started to pray, but instead of me it was the Lord that started talking.

Words like, "Yes, you read it in my Word, I wrote it there, nothing is wrong with it." "But there is something more that I want you to know, I am not the one that is giving the power to Satan." "I want you to have a look at my church." He started rolling something by me, I do not know what I saw but it was about the nastiest thing I ever had to look at. About that time the others started getting to their feet, I did too. I felt like I was in mild shock I guess, but I got the message loud and clear. I have never forgotten it, for one minute. I started trying to do a little better and have not griped at the lord half as much since. God's Church gives Satan all the space he gets on us. That is not God's plan, but it is true.

In around the year sixteen hundred A.D, heyday of the Mystery Babylon Whore, the Mother of Harlots and Abominations of the Earth. There were some mighty good men working on putting together a correct Word of God but it was a good position for one to get himself killed, most of them did. A man named Tyndale, was being burned at the steak for using some of Wycliffe and other's works, while doing some of his own work trying to build a one and complete Word of God.

Mystery Babylon had burned every piece of paper and killed every person that mentioned anything about Jesus or his disciples. Since Constantine had joined the church in somewhere around three-hundred A D, and took over the church that Jesus and the disciples started in Jerusalem. Tyndale's last words coming from the fire, was a prayer to God asking him to move on the King of England, to have an Authenticated Bible written that the man behind a plow could understand it when it was read to him.

Wycliffe's writings had caused much of a stir, but he was dead and had escaped the burning at the steak. The Mystery Babylon church at Rome was so mad they dug up Wycliffe's bones, burned them and sprinkled the ashes in a brook to be carried away, thinking that should kill his influence. They are no smarter than that today, still lying, conniving, killing, trying to force God to make them the only people on earth that he will call his. God is raising ten Antichrist Kingdoms in the Middle East to eat the flesh of Mystery Babylon and burn their city off the earth.

You can look for that to happen, in the not too far future.

A few years after Tyndale's death, King James of Scotland was sent for to sit on the throne of England, a crowd of people met him on the way in, and ask him to give them an authentic, Word of God they could depend on and would unify them. He said he would, told them to form a committee and meet with him when he got set up. Said he knew their problem, he had been fighting the same thing there in Scotland, and together they would work it out.

They did, about seven years later they finished it. In was in the English Language with fifty of the best language scholars that could be found overseeing it, with an order that they all had to come into agreement that it was the best they all could do. That all writings in the world that was named or brought to them would be screened and not ignored but would be sifted through and worked into an approved spiritual book of the writings that could meet the qualifications. And no man was to be left out. I am sure they could tell you why only one man could never have done it.

It was to be put together by the highest scholars in England, but in a low enough language that a man behind the plow could understand it when it was read to him and no man was to be left out. These were the orders that was given to them by King James of England. Around seven years later it was finished, Jesus said, he wrote it, the book was him and he did not want one word changed or moved in it, forever. And we were to preach it to every creature in the earth and to the Greek and the Hebrew. He did not say you can overlook them, they already have their Bibles. He said to preach *this* one to them. Their Bibles were screened and worked into this Bible that Jesus wrote, the books that fit the cannon that was set up. King James sent up to Russia, paid one-half-million dollars for some Scriptures they had. No one was to be left out.

There had been men that had done a lot of good work, some of them are well known in history. None of them had been able to complete the work. Most of them were killed, or driven into hiding.

Their work was gone through and sifted out to use what they could. Jesus said this book will never be killed.

Jesus said a lot of other things in it. Everything Jesus said has, or is coming true to an unbelievable amount of accuracy. While the world has been trying to kill the very memory of him. The world dates every letter it writes and every calendar, from the birth and death of Jesus Christ until today, just a little reminder to Satan. He lost badly, in his encounter with Christ.

If any ancient philosopher had prophesied just a small portion of what Christ has, and it would have come true half as much as Jesus' did, he would be in every school book over the world. What good deed did he do that they purpose to hate him for, until the end of the world? Who did he hurt? Who did he take advantage of, the orphans? The sick and the elderly, the women? How come everybody has heard of him, the world uses his birth and death to date any piece of paper, or calendar from. But very few ever want to talk of him or even be told of him. Even in church, or on Christmas, they do not won't to allow Jesus's name to be used in public places. That takes a lot of nerve, but Satan has a lot of nerve.

As someone I used to know used to say, I guess I'll have to live to be a hundred and fifty years old to figure all that out. Or maybe just read my Bible. It is where I get about all my education. At least I know it is true, when most of the other stuff that comes from man is not.

Most languages are made up of words. It would be impossible for any one person to learn them all. And very difficult for all people to learn just one language. It is the way they started out and the way it is going to end. A person can get a computer now to convert, I suppose, about any language into another. So, if anyone is determined to know God it is far from impossible. But I would recommend anyone to try to get familiar with the English Language. It has been made to contain God's Spiritual Word Language. God's Spiritual Language does not contain the whole English Language of the world, but the opposite, the English Language contains God's Spiritual Language of the world.

Jesus' Word preaches condemnation and destruction unto all the world, and eternal life to all of them that would denounce the world and have nothing in common with it. This put a complete separation between the world's people and God's people. They cannot mix together in the same Spirit, and spirit is the life. The world will not accept Christ nor anything he preached and has grew to hate him more ever generation that it has raised, being taught by Mystery Babylon and the Antichrist, and the ten Muslim nations from the East.

America, the last stand up nation for Jesus Christ on earth, is now putting Christians in jail or worse for the mention of his name on public property. We have Mystery Babylon running our news media and our schools, with a Muslim Antichrist running our government and armed forces. They are trying to, and will unite and will have war between themselves, until the Antichrist Kingdom will eat the flesh of Mystery Babylon and burned her city, there at Rome, off the face of the earth. All we need to do is vote Democrat, they will feed our old folks and children of the Muslim and Antichrist, not of the Christians.

Never mind the debt of Twenty-Trillion dollars that we owe God. A figure bigger than a normal mind can comprehend, not to mention paying it back. I do not believe there is a normal human that even thinks we might pay it back. God teaches we should all pay our debts. Of course, who reads what God says? God has said, if we don't believe what he wrote, we are guaranteed an eternity in hell fire. *Read the next chapter.* Maybe you will understand what we mean by the Spiritual Language that Jesus gave to England, and progressively to the world. It is factually everything needed for the world to know Jesus Christ.

The English Language is under fire because it contains the Spiritual Language of Jesus Christ, it is Jesus Christ. Containing the Godliest papers on earth, including the Bible and our Constitution, and the Declaration of independence. Satan hates it with a passion and has fought to do away with it since it was born in Bethlehem. And our government don't even think enough of it to declare it the official Language of our country. Afraid we will offend the Muslims. And they would have to throw one another in jail.

England took it up and started teaching it, like it said it would do, God made England the most prosperous nation that had every been on the face of the earth. Until Mystery Babylon gradually got into them and taught them out of all of it. They took up Rome's ways again, drove the pilgrims and puritans out of their country, they came to America but brought their Bible with them. America was born out of their movement. Of course, our children don't know the history of that. Mystery Babylon has taken over our country, government and schools and will not let it be taught to our children. Now we are just about gone and there are no new countries left to settle in. We do not seem to have enough sense to know it. And refuse to teach our children or save this one. Why should we, we have Mystery Babylon to do that for us. My, aren't we blessed?!

I think it is high time we awake out of sleep, and let God be heard about, to our children and the world. Everything we know or knew depends on it. And what we teach our children is what they will know.

I have thought about it all very hard and prayerfully, the only hope I can see for us is to rise and take charge and send all of congress home and each state send up replacements to put it back into operation. There is no way we can do it any other way, except take it back the same way they took it from us. Put God back in our schools and throw out any teach that did not want to teach him in. The whole political field are all Devil possessed and protect one another while we are being led into hell with all our family and everything we think we own. We do have an Executive Branch of government now that we can depend on to do the right and lawful and Godly thing.

ENGLAND RECEIVED GOD'S SPIRITUAL LANGUAGE OF THE WORLD.

The Bible was written and given in the English Spiritual Language. Starting out with the request for fifty of the highest English Scholars they could find. I think they ended up with maybe twice that many signed off on it, whatever. But England united and with one sincere heart sought God for a very badly needed Spiritual Book. And God will move completely and thoroughly for such a people that will do that.

Satan is busy until today trying to scatter and shipwreck any substance of the King James Authorized Version of the Bible that Jesus claims openly and completely to be him and his writing, every word of it. Just the fact, that after one-thousand-years, Satan and all the people that are laboring to help him with such dedication, have not been able to put one dent in it, is enough to convince me that every word of it is Jesus Christ, just like he said. Accounts for Satan's attempts to try and degrade or kill the English Language while America refuses to even appoint it to be the official language of our country. Afraid they might offend the Muslims or somebody else, and God forbid we ever do *that!! sic*

Anybody, with the intelligence of an eight-year-old child, that cannot see that no crowd of scholars could be so lucky, as to put so great and renowned book together and one thousand years later it has not had one blemish or correction laid on it. And cannot see that is a miracle, needs help, his elevator doesn't go to the top floor.

I have pity for so many so-called Christians that do not believe God's Word. They surely must be having a constant continuous battle with themselves. God says, them that cannot believe him do not know him, and do not belong to him. I cannot judge them and would not dare try, but I can read God's Word and feel like I am called to teach it to the ones that are willing to hear. I have had many a confused, so called Christian People, to attack me who obviously do not believe God's Word, and seems determined to not change, but desperate to change me.

I could recite several cases, but will narrow it down to just enough to make my point, I hope. One man told me King James would not let certain things be printed in the King James Bible. I told him that everything I had read from anybody that knew anything about it had said, King James had nothing to do with what was wrote in it. Except to gather everything they wanted to view for the experts to attain ever qualifying writings to go into the book. He said to me, --"You know they knew King James well enough that they were not about to put something in there that he would not agree with."

That sounded so good to someone that was wanting to call the scholars and Jesus Christ a liar, which obviously he did, but what could he base it on? How could he prove anything he said? Certainly not by the scholars that translated it, they left quite a bit of an explanation on how they strived to give it their best for it to be a translation, not a writing of any of their own beliefs or feelings. Do you think each of their feelings could be brought into one, or into King James' religion?

They could not prove it by anything Jesus said; he claimed to be the one that wrote it, and that it was even him in his-person. I would be afraid to stake my life against God with carnal reasoning for my backing. We have a world of people that are at ease with carnal reasoning, and don't believe one thing in the Bible that don't agree with what they want to believe. I commune with them about every day. I do not believe Jesus is going to be all that glad to see them on judgment day, calling him a liar. Using carnal reasoning for their substance.

They should read what God thinks of carnal reasoning, they would not be so brave. You can read in the old testament where God zapped off a huge congregation into the earth and flames of fire. Their families, women and kids, their belongings, everything they had went with them, for trying to withstand him and his word from a profit. You could see why there was an inborn fear in mankind in the old days, of an almighty God, he did not fool around with anybody. He has not changed. We are told his Son is much greater than a profit or an angel.

Within a few years of the printing of the Bible, the entire English alphabet received a complete overhaul, mostly in the spelling of words, some letters and sounds of letters were changed and worked out to a miraculous improvement. Some new letters were added to their alphabet, there may have been some words changed, but I do not know of a one. I looked hard and could not find one.

Why would they want to change a word or the meaning of a word because they changed the sound of some letters and added a few new letters? Would it not be simpler just to apply the letters to fit the sound rather than change the sound of the word to try to fit the new sounding letters? Or put in an entirely new word just because some letters were adjusted? I believe people find it amusing to listen to Satan over God, or try to talk for Satan and try to make a fool of God. It seems to make them appear to themselves so smart and confident. I study hard to guard myself against them. I consider them dangerous, and a cheap ticket to hell.

I believe God was greatly impressed and glad to do a complete job for England.

Mostly because they were in earnest and their hearts were united and humble.

It ended up being the one, *United Spiritual Language, to replace the one that the whole world spoke before God confused it from the earth, at the tower of Babel.* The angels, the animals, the people, God said the whole world spoke that one Language. We should have had enough sense to have realized when Jesus said it was the Spirit of God, it was Life, it was the Light, it was the Way, it was our Food to live on, it was the Power of God, it is Jesus Christ himself, containing all the power of God in one Language. To speak it by the Spirit it would remove mountains and cast them into the sea.

I cannot think of all the things he said it was but it was everything we ever might need. Can you think of anything more the first language would do for mankind? Mankind today, still does not realize half the size and value of what it is, not even close. Even though Jesus told us plainly everything it was. And it was for all mankind, no man was left out. What did being another people and speaking a different language than English have, to do with it? --- Not one darn thing.

Let them seek God with as united and earnest a heart as England did and more than probably God would give them a Bible in their Language, but until they do they will have to seek to the English-speaking people to preach this one to them.

And they must have the Spirit to preach the Spirit. Just the Spiritual side of the Language, that can be found wrote in the Word of God. He gave them all different languages to divide them up, once, do you think he would do the same thing to bring them back together, no, but the opposite. It is not Jesus, that is dumb.

I think it would be the reason for the new letters to have them to better cover the words rather than try to make the words cover the letters. But people are so hyper and so prone to think it makes them so smart and sound so intelligent to think they can find a mistake in God or his people and try to make them look foolish, and call them a liar. When they are not even smart enough to see how big a fool they make themselves out to be so much of the time. Carnal always thinks backwards to the Spirit. God does not want to hear carnal reasoning, he knows the Truth.

I had a lady one time, to blast my religion a little, telling me how stupid we were in our Christian beliefs. Said her eight-year old boy came in from school telling her that Jesus could not be the name of Christ. For he had just learned that there was no letter -J- in our alphabet when our Bible was written. He was only eight years old and he figured that out, so she said. (Of course, with help from our atheist school teachers and his atheist mother.) We Christians were a multitude of grown people too dumb to figure it out. I guess there was no *sound* like a J before we got a J in our alphabet. So, sad they could not make the J sound until we put a J in our alphabet. I just kind-of ignored her.

I believed if that was the only thing I could find wrong with someone's religion I would be complementing them, instead of calling them stupid. The world is full of people who wants to think everybody is stupid compared to themselves or their eight-year old son, so what? --- Enjoy it, I guess.

But, there was a mother praising her eight-year old boy for being a fool and a smart-mouth. Do you think that is the way she should be raising and teaching her child? That is exactly what I am talking about. We have lost our children to the Devil and letting them teach us. A smart philosopher once said, "Our very future is founded in the way we teach our children." If he did not say it, he should have, and I just did. Maybe there will be a smart philosopher one day who will say: I heard a dummy say one day----- O' never mind, I'll brag on myself in my next book.

God made the English Language, the main language of the world. Made England the richest, most powerful, nation that had ever been on the earth. Gave the world a printing press around that time.

In around three-hundred years after Christ was crucified over half the known world was confessing Christianity. Christ' disciples had evangelized over half the known world at that time, and did not have the King James Bible. I am sure they had some letters and pieces of Bibles, but all of them was gathered and sifted out everything that could be applied to the King James Bible, including the Greek and Hebrew Bibles. But it was spread mostly by word of mouth, and one on one. It is still the best way to spread the Bible. You will be surprised to see what is done when God is included.

They did it with them being killed and jailed and Mystery Babylon entertaining the world by turning lions and wild dogs and other wild beast loose on Christians wrapped in animal skins in the arena there at Rome for Mystery Babylon's entertainment. It seems to me a strange fact, but Christianity does not grow and spread much without persecution. Word of mouth and one on one takes time.

People do not have the time anymore. We are all just too busy with the cares of this world. And the world telling them how stupid they sound. The world is a good judge of character you know, just look at them. I said something to one of them the other day about character. He looked at me with a puzzled look, and said; "CHARACTER??!!!" I believe they have gone raving mad, I knew he had gone to a Mystery Babylon School.

God has condemned the world since shortly after the creation, and has been preparing himself a small harvest of souls out of it before he is to destroy it entirely and all evidence it ever existed. God has withheld no good thing from them that will believe him and receive him. But has a hell for them that don't.

The world has been trying to kill Christ's followers, since they killed Jesus on the cross. But the harder they tried to kill his influence the more it grew, it was like a wild fire, the harder they stomped the more it spread. This is what has separated the world and God's people, until they have nothing in common together. Look over the world and into it, study correct history, the Bible is the best history book ever written, if you cannot see this, you are blind like God has said. He recommended one church to use some eye salve, I've been told their town was famous for the eye salve they produced, I do not know, I have never been there.

I do not mean to be offensive in using the term blindness so much it is a term Jesus used very often. We should keep in mind

Jesus was always speaking in and from a spiritual point of view. He is all Spirit and always talking from and about the spiritual side of things. After giving his carnal body for a sacrifice for us. As he is, so is everybody that is born again into his Spirit. There is a way, we can hear the spiritual allocation, if we get our Spiritual eyes and ears opened. If we do not, we cannot see anything in the Bible with any understanding.

We are not talking about one's person or his carnal side in any way shape or form. Jesus said in some things we offend them all, but woe unto the one through which the offence comes, in other words, God's people just don't need to be taking offence at anything, if we can help it, but offenses will come. The world will hate you so bad, they will kill you and think they are doing God a favor.

We just need to get our Spiritual eyes open and see truth as the best we possibly can. If it is truth we need to face it, do the best we can to improve any bad situation. If it is a lie it is always best to let God handle it, and he will. Truth is the only thing we must have to stand on to battle it with. The world itself is a lie. Truth will always prevail in the end.

If you are afraid someone is not going to believe it just keep in mind I have found people will believe things very much the way they want to believe them, usually the way that is profitable to them. Sometimes even see the things the way they want to see them, regardless of how they happened.

There will not be much you can do about it if they don't want to believe it, or putting their own spin on it. Like I say the truth will come out usually quicker than you think. This was around sixteen-hundred AD when England had broken from the Mystery Babylon Whore, that got its real beginning when Constantine Joined Christianity in around three-hundred AD for the purpose to take it over and did. England decided to seek God with a whole heart for a true Spiritual Word of God. God gave them the Bible over one thousand years ago, Jesus Christ in Spiritual Word Form.

The Emperor Constantine found he could not win a fight against the church, so he joined it and been in it and running it ever since.

I searched diligently and did not find a word that had been changed or added or removed from the so called new Bible, but Satan loves to shout it in everybody's ears that it was rewritten, I have been told, five times, since Jesus wrote it. But I could not find the evidence, you can believe Satan if you prefer, your privilege, but I prefer to believe Jesus Christ. We have a world full of people that just loves to interrupt you when you say something like I am writing here. And just swear that the Bible has been rewritten many times, and I know they do not know any more about it than I do, just what somebody else told them, mostly Satan, and his people loves it. Calling Christ, a liar, about it having been changed. I cannot judge them but I think they are skating on some mighty thin Ice.

I do not believe a man can call Jesus a liar and remain a Christian without repentance. I see no room for them in the scriptures. Again, I am not a judge but can read my Bible and told to believe it. That book is still standing, and like it says, any people that will pick it up and obey it, will be blessed above any people on the earth. Like England did, then America did. It has never failed any people in the one thousand years it has existed, and never will. This, is why every person on this earth that does not want to believe it, will hate it because it will destroy and cast into hell any people that works against it. And will eventually get them that just ignore it.

From the time the colonies started up, Mystery Babylon has desired to kill and conquer our Country, fought against us in two world wars. When it became plain we were going to win, they made some big strides to try and convince us they were on our side all the time and been trying to ride us. I have stated they are not a beast, but a beast rider. Of course, we fell for it, both times. Which side do you think Germany and Italy was on? Which side is Mystery Babylon on now, not the side of the Bible for sure.

Mystery Babylon is not a beast, but a beast rider. And is going to be riding the seven-headed beast till its final day. It is in Rome today but riding America into the ground; right now, tearing down every statue from our past it can, in order, to bury anything pointing to our history. They have removed American History from our schools some years ago. Some of our high school kids did not know the name of our first president, or who won world war II. This generation has not noticed it since they are not concerned with what our kids are taught. You can tell that by how they act. They never have cared, not even for the last several generations until today.

The reason being is Mystery Babylon hates anything about Jesus Christ. He is the Bible, and our history is full of it. They have finally figured it out, they cannot touch us, if we hold up the Bible.

America is not standing with the Bible anymore, as a country, and is going downhill fast. Mystery Babylon is making big strides now, to mount the Muslim beast, and will, but it has not been broken to ride. God is the only one that will always deal with anything for what it is, and he is never fooled or unfair. Had they rather let a Democrat settle it, or maybe a Republican? Or perhaps a liberal, or maybe a conservative? Maybe a Catholic or a Baptist? Which one would give all sides a square deal and everybody would be content with it?

Not a one will, except God. And no one can be on God's side without believing the Bible I believe we should all come together and agree to let God settle it, told about in the Word of God and we can all get a fair and balanced deal. That is what the Bible is all about, and the purpose of having church meetings is to study it. It will only work if we can come together as one in agreement with the Bible, it will work ever time if we can learn how it says to read, believe, and trust God.

One may not get everything he wants, but it is the only way everybody will get a fair and balanced deal, and come into one body and be blessed. I do not buy in on the teaching that each man can believe the Bible any way he pleases. That is among the most foolish carnal statements I believe any man can make. It would be dangers to turn a man like that loose with a Bible. He could never be used to work for the Lord Jesus Christ. He is worse off than a denomination that thinks they are the only one that can understand it right. The Bible teaches the Bible is the only one that can interpret the Bible. Nothing else can qualify, this is the reason for so many disagreements that seems like so many people cannot settle. Man does not qualify to settle them, only the Bible can. But it does tell man how.

The Devil has men like that working on every corner in the name of the Lord. While giving God blame for all his failures rather than admit that he does not have the mind of Christ and does not know the Truth nor how to preach the Word of God from the Spirit. This may sound like a little heavy handed to some but I believe it is just the way Christ said and wrote it, and just the way it is. I do not feel eligible or called to preach it any other way. What does the world hate it for? Ever ask yourself why?

I favor the Word of God just the way it is wrote, and the way God said to establish it. Anybody can have, *"anointed"* wrote on the front of any book that he has wrote. But he will have to have it published under his own name. It will have to be wrote by Christ, or a direct copy of, to be registered under Christ's name, or as the King James Authorized Translation. Or somebody could be in legal trouble if his name is not, Jesus Christ. If it is registered under the name Jesus Christ the Son of God it should be quoted just the way Jesus wrote it, or it will not qualify as God's Word.

Anybody that has read this far is bound to have some interest in this. I have been trying to build up to some startling facts that will be hard for some people to follow, and they probably won't if they do not do some studying and verifying but that will just have to be up to them. But some of these things coming up, all through this book, I have never heard preached in my forty years of working for the lord.

I have written a book on "Mystery Babylon," and one on "The Mark of the Beast" some of this I may be laying out from these books. But I believe any of it you can establish from the Bible. Like God said to do. I have said a little in all my books about God taking the one Language from the earth causing great confusion among the humans it is still here today. Nations are pretty well built around their languages God did that for a purpose, but it has served its purpose.

God knows the end is almost here and there are not going to be a huge number of people left that is interested in God's plan in gathering his people together for the millennial reign where he will reign from Jerusalem for a thousand years when he turns back to the Jews. But that is where everything is headed. Might as well get on board, it probably will not help carnality much. But may very well save your Spiritual soul. And will take care of your carnality. That is the part of us that is not eternal.

When one talks about eternal things, he is talking about Godly things. When he talks about Godly things he is talking about eternal things. Of course, God can change the form of anything, the way he wants to. He said in one place, "What I make, I make to last forever." A soul is a live spirit God built inside a fleshly house. The fleshly house fell from God and is going back to the dust from which it came. The spirit God gave it will go back to God.

You must make the choice for your soul, go into the Spirit of God and live forever or go with the fallen spirits of Satan into an everlasting place of punishment and darkness. If you choose the Spirit of God, he will give you a new body. If you choose to go without God's Spirit, it appears to me you will not have a body. I suppose you will have to depend upon the one you chose as your God to get you around. Like the government I guess. A lot of people will be crying for Obama, but he will not have a body either. A harsh price to pay for enjoying a few years of being able to do as one pleases, being his own God so to speak. At least feeling like it. Better pick a God that will be able to help you in eternity, and will not lie to you.

People that have been Devil possessed, should know a little about what that is like. Even if you like it, look at what you will have to contend with when God's Spirit is gone from the world. See all the killing and torcher that is going on today, every day, all around us? Seems like that is enough to make one sick and we have laws trying to stop it. I wonder what kind of laws Satan will have to protect a helpless human being's soul that he hates? When one moves into an eternity where there is none of God's laws there to protect one. And God's Spirit is gone.

All the working parts of the body is to keep the flesh alive and going, the spirit and soul does not need them until the Spirit is gone. God built them to last forever, built the flesh to house and carry them around for maybe seventy years or so. We should appreciate it as we have the body but not get too attached to it for it is temporary and dead to the Spirit when God calls his Spirit back, who is going to be the one to move it around?

Talking about a body, I believe ours is very handy, enough that the spirits that are thrown out from God for rebellion, seek constantly to make their dwelling in one of them. And has taken every opportunity to take advantage of them, until God put a stop to them moving into one at their own convenience now they must get at least a certain amount of your permission with their lies and persuasive tactics. God says two strong spirits cannot spoil the goods in the same house. Only a fool would believe them, but we have a lot of fools. Seems like more every day. People that follow a good feeling religion, I guess.

I am trying to get this around to the hereafter life. I have not read where God or Satan have promised the ones that miss heaven, a new body. I do not read where a spirit has a body except an image of one, and I don't know of him having to use one like we do. I know we have great preachers and book writers that make a big issue of the Bible speaking a lot about God's parts, have you ever shaken Jesus' hand physically, or know anyone that has since he went back to being a Spirit? Or maybe before? Not that he can't fake ever handshake he wants to but it is for sure it in not a common thing. I just assume he just does not have a need to.

Jesus is available to everyone but it is for sure any communication will be in and by the Spirit of God. If you refuse his Spirit, I will not concede you know very much about him. He is a Spirit, and cares very little about the carnal part of anything.

The Spirit that you chose when you were living down here on the earth will be the only one I see to move you around, when the Spirit of God leaves this earth. A carnal spirit is contrary to Christ and is going to burn in an everlasting fire, after the battle of Armageddon. I would not look forward toward any such eternity. God has given us a choice, man thinks he knows best. One day he will see, God has not told us one lie. And he is not going to save anybody that cannot believe him, for it is truth that saves one. All he has promised to them that cannot believe him, is an eternity in hell. That is all Satan has, to offer anyone.

I have been trying to explain all through my books, God is the Father of Truth, Satan is nothing but the father of lies. The ones that do not know Christ are the Devil's children. Christ will not claim them, he is not a thief, but will not let the Devil steel a one of his. And is well able to care for the ones that is raised up unto him. He will allow the Devil to try and temp each one of us, but no more than any of us can bare. With every temptation, he will provide a way of escape. The ones that are not his, are walking on shaky legs, or hoping around on his one left leg. (I do not think much of the left; some whole days go by that I do not think of them at all).

Any American that has been blessed with common sense and one eye that is open. Must know that our country has been intentionally run into the ground at least double in the past ten years than it has been in any time since its birth. Even including the Civil War days, God did not let them get this low, Spiritually or financially. Our politicians were not all millionaires.

There is plenty of blame to go all the way around, but you can read the twenty-eighth chapter of the book of Deuteronomy in God's Word. With a little thought and attention, I will promise, you can see every reason we are what we are, with the remedy plainly given in the same chapter.

I once heard a doctor say, ("In order, for one to get well, one must quit doing what one is doing that is making him sick.") The Democrats completely took charge in the last two years of Bush's last term. With lies and lying promises, and fraud elections with illegal, stolen, paid for votes by the millions. Which is all our fault, we allowed it, the left was ready to claw your eyes out if you mentioned them. God has said we should never believe or tell a lie. But that will not matter when it comes to correcting our mistakes and gaining our recovery, only the lessons we should learn from the experiences and God's Word. God always gives us the rulers we want and *deserve.* God's book has every answer. And it is in his Word, the Bible, if we will just look it up. Written in a Spiritual Language.

I know that may offend some of you atheist, and a few dozen organizations that you have formed and enjoying many rich and powerful political members, and taxpayers and Soros's money. To be quite frankly honest with you, I really, just do not give a rat's ear what they think of it. It is high time the people that love our Country and the liberty our God and Constitution grants to us, pick themselves up and stand for the Truth and what is right. They are listed in God's Word. We are going to be forced to wake up and protect it if we want to keep it.

I, for one am ready, and we should not have to pay the politicians money for it. I do not see as we owe them a thing. God may not be a Democrat or a Republican, but I would bet my life on it that he darn sure is not a left headed liberal and he is always right, and never a liar. He judges by one's fruit, not the name you choose are how much of the countries money one can spread around with his lies. Money that does not belong to one, and used to gain power.

I see no fruit from a Liberal, but robbery and destruction. Passing out trillions of dollars of taxpayer's money like feeding a bunch of fattening hogs, mostly lying news reporters and billion-heirs to lie for them. And pay punks to riot for him and try to wreck our glorious country. And trying to kill the few sensible people that are left in the world. Just yesterday I heard a news commentator bragging about how much better a salesman Obama was than Trump. I do not know how a man can be a good salesman without being a liar.

The sad part of it is, how many grown voters does not know, Obama and his crowd, sold ten trillion dollars of our money that we did not have, plus maybe that much more that they collected and stole and committed for us. How good a salesman does it take to sell money that does not belong to him? Voters should have more sense than that, WHAT is WRONG with them, we do not need that brand of salesman. Only a lying Democrat or a scared to death established Republican, would call him *good*.

People believe what they want to believe, regardless of the facts, is one thing wrong. Obama spreading ten-trillion dollars of the working man's tax dollars for the next three generations, the left sure wanted to think that was good. That only meant to me they got their shire of it. I do not know how much longer God is going to carry us for what our forefathers did so long ago. But I really do believe not for much longer. When he quits we are going to drop like an anvil, a sure bet.

God is running this world since it was formed by his word. And has always tried to care and work with man without withholding one good thing from us. As a fact, it was his word that created it, and money grows nothing but evil. Of course, he doesn't always agree with us what is good for us, but lets us have it after warning us and trying to work with us on what we need to do. But even God's patience wears thin after a while, after our Godly character and respect for him has disappeared. We will reap what we have sown.

Man, by himself cannot make good decisions, this, is why he is always in trouble, and wrong and must have the Bible in some form, to lead and correct himself to stay straight. I've seen pastors running a church, preaching with seldom ever opening his Bible. Too much confidence in himself, and too much preaching the same thing over and over. It does not need to be changed to fit the changing times, another one of Satan's lies. God has not changed, and never will. But it can use a little broadening and deeper preaching. Who do they want to please, a changing world of people or a none changing God? What was not tolerated in Moses' time, God will not tolerate today. I think that may be called a little of "Keeping up with the Jones." Jesus died to give us a little more time, and help.

Look what the People have changed into in these last few years, who wants that? God has said, he doesn't, and is going to prove it. If one does not believe God then I guess he has nothing to worry about, until judgment. I may not be the smartest man in the world, but I can read my Bible and look at the horizon, and add two and two, and I believe God.

These people that says there is no God, but want to curse and blame him for everything, makes no sense. That, two and two, does not add up to four for me nor does it add up to common sense. When people throw-out common sense, they throw-out God in the same act. God is common sense. I do not care how cheap something else is, I do not want to buy it at any price. It is a rock that will roll only for Satan and his greedy fools.

As one lives his life here on this earth, reaches the age of accountability, he will be judged on which side he chooses to serve. The side of righteousness or the side of free-lance with the Devil. With God, there is no hung-in-between. Just a thin line on either side of us that we don't want to get caught over on the wrong side of. Christ will be the one to judge, he has said it will be with all things considered. Much of it will be on the amount of light one has been showed and seen, received or rejected. Only you and Christ will know all that. But Christ has promised he will be fair according to his Word.

I was once told by a preacher of several-years, that all people would be one of the two, saved or unsaved, and everyone on each side would receive the same reward. That is just not all the way true, maybe the first half of that statement. If it was all true, I feel like I could disregard about half my Bible and not need it. I am not ready for that. If I can understand anything about God's Word, each person will receive his own reward, and face his own record. I do not believe man has enough wisdom to talk about judgement, past what is stated in God's Word, and that being established by two and three witnesses.

Christ is going to burn up the entire creation with every soul whose name is not written in the Lamb's Book of Life, because man is not able to get himself serious about the Words of Jesus Christ. I am not smart at all but I can understand why, man can come up with some of the most ridiculous ideas, I can hardly imagine where he gets them from. One could sound much smarter to just try to stick with what Jesus says. It is for sure Jesus does not need man to do his thinking for him, or explain God's word to him. God's Word explains God Word. Only somebody that does not know Jesus could come up with such an idea that Jesus Christ needs our help.

I would suggest you not get too skiddiest at my using the expression, I believe, or, I think, and similar remarks, you can rest assured I lean heavy on such remarks after much studying and research, and use the Bible for all my foundation. I invite you very soundly to check me out very thoroughly, as that is much of my intention, is to stir up some interest and get some attention in that direction.

Language is among the biggest words in the world, it can cover about all the people of the earth. If one can speak enough of them. I believe the spirits are about as strange to our languages as we are to theirs. I believe the spirits still speak the same language as all the earth was speaking before God confused it from the earth. Every man had to come up with a language for his group to communicate within his circle. I believe they all communicated mind to mind without necessarily making a carnal sound before God took it from the earth. Can you hear two spirits talking today? Reckon they just do not talk any longer? How did the snake and Eve have a conversation?

I also doubt if many spirits can speak as we do without borrowing a voice box of some sort from some person or thing. This could explain many things in the Word of God to see and understand this.

67

If you cannot communicate with the Spirit of God, in your mind, you are missing out on the very communicating with God, and you must do a lot of soul searching and guessing and learning by trial and error. And trying out a lot of things you see and hear from other people. A good and costly way to learn about how so many people can lie and believe a lie.

I find it very interesting how people treat languages today. I deal with people all the time that are trying to get ahead in the world and can see how they are afraid to use the name Jesus Christ in their conversation. And are trying to get it outlawed. I reckon they think it makes them look stupid and weak to the world to sound a little religious. They rather mock, laugh at, sound too smart, tuff, and above anything that sounds like a reference to a God that is above man.

That is one of Satan's missions, he works very hard at it. A newspaper will just about not print an article in their paper if it sounds very religious. And you cannot hardly blame them for the whole world is waiting to attack them with any damaging remarks they can get away with, to make themselves look bigger and smarter and above Jesus Christ. Christians included, they are ashamed of Christ while claiming to be good Christians on Sunday Morning, if they have time. I guess they think that God does not see them except on Sunday Morning. God says we are the ones that are asleep and blind, not him.

God is a language that Satan hates and would like to do away with. Including the whole English Language, for the Bible that Jesus wrote is from the English Language, so is the Declaration of our Independence, the Constitution and about any other Godly written document that has any significance.

Why do you think anybody that is ate up with the world wants to use all the dirty, filthy words he can come up with and mix the word God in them everywhere he can? Or the word mother. It shows how much they favor speaking for Satan rather than God. I think they think it makes them look tuff and strong to themselves and the world.

Study God's Word, we are told to establish things by the Word of God. It is the final judge on everything here and the hereafter, and will never be changed. Does not that make the Word of God a very valuable thing? It is Jesus Christ, if you cannot believe that, you just missed him.

People do not want, or have the capability, to grasp the smallest end of the facts. God is going to totally disintegrate the creation and everything that is attached to it. Including all mankind that has not been born again into his Spirit. Some of these facts have been somewhat laid back for centuries, but have been revealed to us plainer as time has went by. As sin doth abound, so does grace. As God has warned us and showed the ones that have been seeking him, everything has been moving faster and faster on the overall scale, especially as we are entering these last days. God said everything that can be shaken will be shook off. God has said he would send an angel through the sky to warn his people to come out of Mystery Babylon before he destroys her. (In the twenty-fourth Ch. Of Matt. Is the plainest place for this to happen) If we do not want to partake of her plagues, but people that do not know God will not hear the angel. Why we should know the Spiritual Language, and read our Bible.

If you want to find him, you can do that by prayerfully studying the Word and seeking a good man of God to help. You can know them by their fruit. Jesus said that not everybody that says Lord, Lord, will enter in with his people, and may not lead you straight. The ones that will, are getting scarce by the day. One must get to know the Spirit of God. He is the one we all must follow. There are probably millions of fakes but only one Spirit of God. It says we will be accountable for every idle word we use. Man, also has two sides, the spiritual side and the carnal side. God is only interested in the spiritual side. The other side is dead.

People can't seem to realize that God has a big hand in everything that happens to each of us and everything that does not happen to us. We all worry about God keeping us happy. We need to keep him happy with us and we cannot do that with worldly things, or being happy with the world. God needs nothing this world does offer. He already owns it all and going to destroy it when its time is up. Our inventions are what he doesn't want, they are what are going to destroy us. If we will live close to God, we will not need a one of them. Elijah, got around very well, and when necessary, very fast, without a car or plane. I doubt if he ever learned to drive one.

Man is determined to get ahead of God in everything. Look around at man, he doesn't seem to know that God exist up front of and above him. I believe it will be a shock to most men when they find out he is still in the front, and has been running things all along. And never really needed them at any time. But we do need each other and him to survive. You can see that if you can just get one Spiritual eye open.

GOD IS STILL RUNNING THINGS, AND WILL FULFILL EVERYTHING HE HAS SAID.

I have thought several times I have finished this book, but have not been able to get the ends gathered up and the publishing started, so I just keep on writing on it. Just now the big flood is going on down in Texas and up the coast. God has given me a book of revelations on it, I've been reluctant on getting started on it. It is hard to know where to start, but seems like it fits to start on the end of this book, here goes. How many of these facts can anyone deny that they are plain truths?

I have made plain, if I read it in my Bible, plainly identified and established, to me it is a Truth. God is in complete control of the weather and he will use it drastically to reprove humanity, or to get their attention. God says he has his way in the whorl wind. And anywhere else he chooses. God has made it plain this nation is a chosen nation of God, built and protected and blessed by his very hand. Declared by our forefathers to be one nation under God with "In God we trust" on every piece of money we have printed or stamped.

This eats at the heart and soul of Satan and all the people he has possessed, or them that have any other god than the God of the creation. They are eaten up with hate at the mention of Christ's name. God has named them Mystery Babylon and the Antichrist Kingdoms of the East. Two of the three Evil Spirits John saw in the sixteenth chapter of Revelations, Satan being the third. The two will contain every person whose name is not in the Lambs Book of Life, when Christ throws them all into the lake of fire at the end of the world.

What are some of the biggest problems that Satan and his imps are causing us today? They have this country so divided, broken up, and ate up with some of the lowest sins mentioned in God's word. We are being physically attacked throughout our country, and on every border. By some of the most ungodly people in the world, even threating us with *civil war* on our own soil while killing Christians every day. The same party has already tried that once, and anxious to try it again. They are determined to conquer this country. If they can bury our "Bible" they will have it done. And they know it.

The invading forces are pouring in over our borders in the south by the millions. We know they will vote Democrat along with tens and tens of thousands of dead, and paid for and other illegal voters. So, the liberals are fighting to keep our borders open at any coast, assuring the elections to go for the Christ hating Democrat liberals. Trump managed to get enough of the polls cleaned up a little, enough to win the last election. Surprising the Left, they thought they had it sealed up again carefully planned. Anybody that could not see what the democrats stand for after having Obama over us for eight years.

Let me see if I can name just a few of them. He spoke an order against the Supreme Court's ruling twice that this is a Christian nation, saying it was not anymore. They gave one person a long term in prison with trumped up chargers, because he was campaigning for the right to own a gun. Court-martialed a Military Chaplin and kicked him out of the service for praying in Jesus's name. Ordering and threating all other solders for using the name Jesus while in uniforms. Made every ruling, every speech, every decision he ever made while in office that I ever heard in favor of the Muslims.

The word went out plainly, no Bible was to be found on or in a school property, some teachers were fired when a Bible was found in their possession on the school property. The Koran was to be taught in the classroom under the name of a culture, while enjoying the privilege of religious freedom protection. Not that I care or did not know, but it was noticeable that every time he referred to the Koran, it was the Holy Koran, when he spoke of the Bible it was just Bible. Many more things but I would run out of paper before I run out of them.

I think he hated Christ dearly, and the Democrats loved him for it. I quit the Democrats better than forty years ago for that very reason. They have gotten so much worse since then, I believe they are in a conspiracy, even with foreign governments, that they are determined to put this country completely under. They just about have it done. And Trump's hands are tied until he can get some sensible judges on our court's benches, and some college professors that are not Devil possessed. I don't believe they are going to let him do it. We have too many Republicans that I cannot see why they call themselves Republicans, if I could afford it, I would mail them a big D. to put in front of their name. Or try to have them arrested for masquerading as someone they are not. Of course, we have a lot of voters that are the same way. And I am sure they know them and Soros' money. Where is Trump's lawyers? If it is against the law for another government to meddle in our elections, why is it not against the law for Soros to contribute ten million dollars to Hillary's election, do you think he might have been trying to influence that election? I wonder how much he donated to the Republican congressmen to vote Democrat?

I think the looser and some of her supporters cried all night, must have been painful to get such a shock. God says he gives us every one of our rulers. People that do not know him have a hard time believing him on that one, or anything else for that matter. They swore to recall the election and to impeach Trump one way or the other. They have tried everything they can pull to set on him, keeping him down hoping he can do nothing, and look bad to the people. I believe God got disgusted with them and decided a little of the border needed shut down for a while and cleaned up a little. God knows how to close and wash a border and has sent a few hundred miles of rain water that is impassible on the ground leaving it there long enough for us all to have a look at. I think maybe we ought to look at it and take in some of the facts. God has promised many more things if we don't.

California is so far left, they have got clean off the board. I have been predicting for around thirty to forty years that God is going to dump them off into the ocean. But I believe he may be going to burn it up a little at a time. Along with a few dozen other natural disastrous, you would think they would notice. Is not that section of Texas that was washed away, close to the area where there was a movement to set up Sharia law? God has said man is a blind and stubborn creature.

They try to claim Trump is so ungodly to not throw our borders open to any religion on earth, with some of the worst Christ hating people in the world. What is ungodly about not giving our goods to the ungodly or them that are worshiping false gods, and vowed to kill all Christians from the earth? God said to put them to death, their women, children, old and young, to not let them dwell among you. Not to mention take complete charge of you and try to kill you're God.

The Bible says if someone comes to you with any other doctrine other than Jesus Christ and he crucified, do not let them into your house. If you give him God speed you will be partakers of his evil deeds. God says to mark them which cause division and offences contrary to the doctrine of Christ and he crucified, and avoid them. Having a form of godliness but denying the power thereof from such turn away, we are to guard the doctrine. Jesus said to not cast your perils before swine. They would trample them under foot, turn and rend you to pieces. And many other such things God says. Do you think he was talking about hogs?

This is still a Christion nation under God, despite of what the Muslim Democrat, Mystery Babylon party says. We are not to receive them as brethren. They have not stolen us completely, yet, and cannot, unless we just give it to them. Which is what it looks like we are doing. Can we not read God's Word? He says to read it.

You will know why them Devil worshipers hate it, they are scared of it.

I had a man tell me once that the Bible says I was not to mention the word politics from the pulpit. I have not found what Bible he was reading from. It must have been written by Satan himself. It was surely not from my King James Authorized Bible. Politics is the biggest false religion we must deal with in this country. They have made of themselves, a religion. I have been threatened for mentioning politics from the pulpit more than once. It came from Democrats. I had about as soon sign my name up for the ISIS draft as to vote for a Democrat.

If we allow them to take our Bible we will be helpless, we might as well take their "Mark of the Beast" and prepare for an eternity in hell with the Devil being our only way around. After all, where would we be going? No person will survive denying or ignoring Jesus Christ. He is life to anyone who knows him. We are told to look to his mighty works and fear him.

The storm in Texas is a perfect example. It is amazing at the damage, and yet so many lives were spared. The ones he did spare was willing to go to work. God would rather we were willing to go to work without having to wash away everything we owned and worked for. The big are the same as the small when God moves, just the big should have been caring the bigger load. God says he gives us gifts according to our several abilities; does he not give us abilities according to our gifts?

People need to read their Bible, it is Jesus Christ that is pouring out the wrath of God on the world, to plead with man to repent, in the sixteenth chapter of Rev. in the last week of years promised us in Daniel. Some of the times, like man has never seen before, and will never have to see again. People can do a lot of harsh things out of love. Jesus is the one that has told us these things. Maybe when one gets scorched with the sun for a five-month period, blood and hail laying all around, many people being killed, maybe some will believe him then. If they have taken the Mark, it will cost them their lives here on earth.

Washing away a streak out of one of our larger states don't seem to have shook up our people much, maybe a little. Jesus is going to be the one that throws the Antichrist, and the Mystery Babylon Whore, with every soul whose name is not written in the Lambs Book of Life into the lake of fire that burns forever and forever. I believe man should fear him a little. Seems everything God builds, has two sides, I believe I will try to be on Jesus's loving side. He has told us now is the time to get there. Everybody is welcome.

ABOUT THE AUTHOR

Billy Wilson grew up in North Central Arkansas. He has been a pastor for approximately forty years and is currently the pastor at Lute Mountain Community Church. Billy, father of four and grandfather to thirteen, resides in Shirley, Arkansas, with his wife, Linda. This is his fourth book.